Some Somerset Country Houses

FOLLOWING PAGE

Dillington House, the west front.

ROBERT DUNNING

Some Somerset Country Houses

THE DOVECOTE PRESS

First published in 1991 by The Dovecote Press Ltd
Stanbridge, Wimborne, Dorset BH21 4JD
ISBN 0 946159 85 8

© Robert Dunning

Designed by Humphrey Stone

Photoset in Palatino by
The Typesetting Bureau Ltd, Wimborne, Dorset
Origination by Chroma Graphics (Overseas) Pte Ltd, Singapore
Printed and bound by Kim Hup Lee Printing Co Pte Ltd, Singapore

Contents

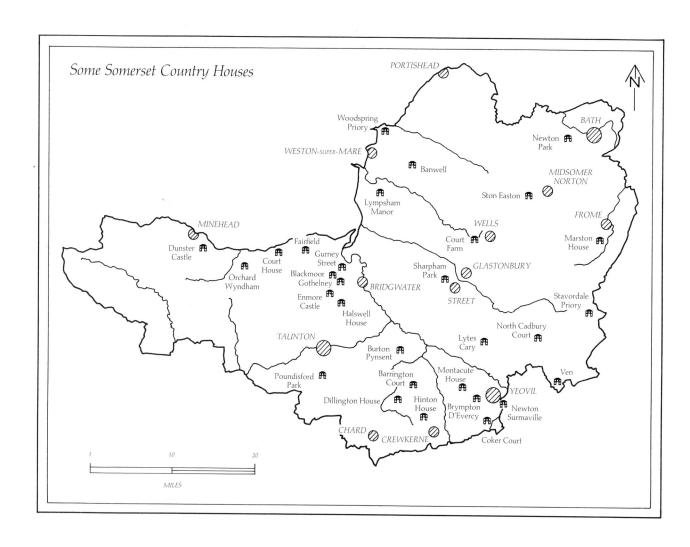

Some Somerset Country Houses

PORTISHEAD

BATH

Woodspring
Priory

Newton
Park

WESTON-super-MARE

Banwell

MIDSOMER
NORTON

Lympsham
Manor

Ston Easton

FROME

MINEHEAD

WELLS

Marston
House

Dunster
Castle

Fairfield

Court
Farm

GLASTONBURY

Court
House

Gurney
Street

Sharpham
Park

Orchard
Wyndham

Blackmoor
Gothelney

STREET

Stavordale
Priory

BRIDGWATER

Enmore
Castle

Halswell
House

North Cadbury
Court

TAUNTON

Lytes
Cary

Ven

Burton
Pynsent

Montacute
House

Poundisford
Park

Barrington
Court

YEOVIL

Dillington House

Hinton
House

Brympton
D'Evercy

Newton
Surmaville

CHARD

CREWKERNE

Coker Court

1   10   20

MILES

Acknowledgements

My first and greatest debt is to the owners of the houses included in the book. Without their support and unfailing kindness it would have been impossible. Not only have they allowed their homes to be studied and photographed, but they have also provided me with a great deal of information.

I am particularly grateful to Anthony Kersting for taking so many of the superb photographs that illustrate the book. He has battled with the weather, geography and time, often visiting the same house again and again to obtain the exact photograph I had asked for.

I am also grateful to the following for their help: the rector of Hinton St George, the Reverend John King, and the vicar of St Decuman's, Watchet, Prebendary Michael Barnet, for permitting memorials in their churches to be photographed; Sir Mervyn Medlycott for both information and help with illustrations; Michael McGarvie, Peter Hopkins, Roger Saul and David Bromwich for help with illustrations; A.P. Baggs, Peter Bird, Gerard Leighton, and John and Jane Penoyre for architectural information; Jeremy Dunning for photographic assistance; and David Burnett, an encouraging, patient and persistent publisher.

ROBERT DUNNING
Taunton

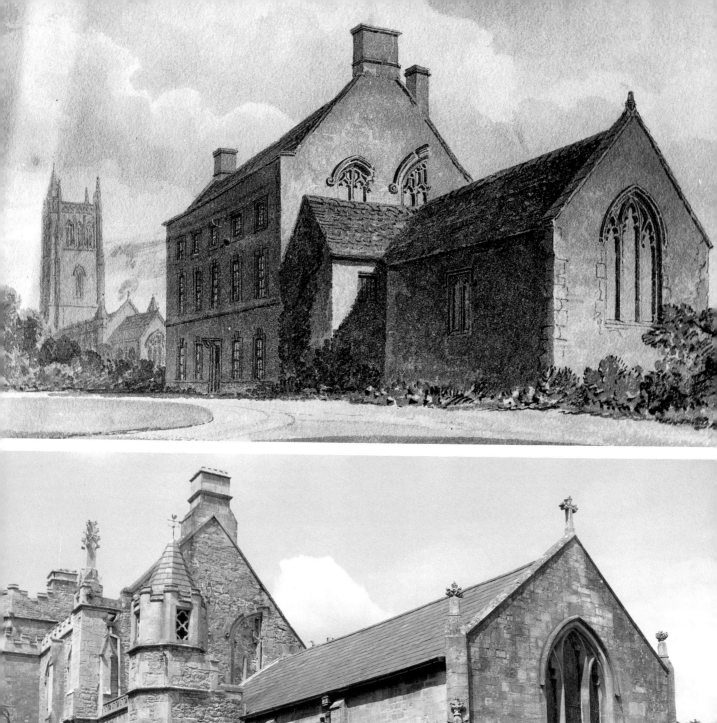

The Country House

Top. Banwell. A wash drawing by J.C. Buckler dated 1827 showing the remains of Bishop Bekynton's manor house, incorporated in a later house known as Banwell Abbey or Banwell Court.

Bottom. Banwell Abbey. Much of the apparently medieval detail is by Hans Price c.1870.

Abbot Richard Bere, the powerful abbot of Glastonbury, was appointed to his high and mighty office at the end of 1493. Ten years later the great survey of abbey estates which bears the name 'Abbot Bere's Terrier', declared that the park of Sharpham measured 382 acres and that in it stood a manor house 'of his own new and sumptuous construction, comprising manor, chapel, parlour, chambers, storehouses, kitchen and other rooms and offices'. Here was a house, in the moors north of the abbey's village of Walton and not many miles west of Glastonbury, where Bere evidently sought seclusion from his brethren, a place where he could be seen to be the lord of the wide acres which the abbot of Glastonbury had so obviously become, a place to entertain his guests with a little hunting, or simply to survey from his house on the hillock the fertile moors which were the source of much of Glastonbury's wealth.

It was at this same house in the fateful autumn of 1539 that the King's Visitors sought out Abbot Richard Whiting, Bere's successor, 'to call to his remembrance that which he had forgotten to confess to them on their previous visitation and so declare the truth'. The truth was evidently not acceptable. The abbey fell to the Crown, and with it Sharpham, and a few weeks later Whiting himself, having been brought back from London, was tried at Wells, dragged through Glastonbury, and hanged with two of his fellow monks on the Tor.

The abbey estate included many manor houses where abbots might well have retired on occasion. John Selwood, abbot 1457-93, is said to have built 'a noble mansion' with 'chapel, hall, sumptuous apartments and magnificent porch' at East Brent, though how often he used it is not known, and the house does not survive. For Bere and Whiting Sharpham was the favourite home away from cloister and business, a country house where they might retreat from the pressures that an abbot of Glastonbury was heir to.

Other heads of religious houses might well have had their preferred residences. John Cantlow, prior of Bath, seems to have cared especially for Widcombe, away from smells of the city: he contributed to the building of the church tower and was buried in the church after his death in 1499.

The bishops of Bath and Wells, seculars not confined (even in theory) to their cloister, were not usually in the 15th century to be found staying too long at their Palace at Wells, for their presence tended to make the Dean and Chapter nervous and irritable. Each bishop had his own favourite residence in the diocese. Henry Bowet (1401-8) seems to have preferred Banwell, Nicholas Bubwith (1408-24), John Stafford (1425-43) and Thomas Bekynton (1443-65) Banwell or Wookey. The house called Banwell Abbey, and Court Farm at Wookey contain fragments of these two episcopal houses, the former repaired by Bekynton, and where he planted what was described as a 'splendid' orchard. Court Farm was probably begun by Bishop Jocelin of Wells in the earlier 13th century and was altered by Bekynton in the 15th.

Wookey, Banwell, Sharpham and perhaps Widcombe were country homes, chosen by their temporary owners in preference to other urban residences; escapes from the hurly-burly of their busy official lives. Necessarily, they could not be handed down to any but their successors in office. They were not investments for progeny although they were, for so long as they were occupied, centres of social and political influence. They bore some of the characteristics of country houses but not all, yet in them, perhaps, the origins of the country house may be discerned.

The sale or division of the estates of the bishops of Bath and Wells and the Dissolution of the Monasteries changed the scene, opening a huge land market and bringing new elements into play. Tudor merchants seem to have had a compulsive desire to invest in land, for it represented security not to be guaranteed in every voyage, and built their new houses on virgin sites chosen for their aesthetic qualities. Ancient families converted their castles to something more approaching domesticity, but they remained castles, sited for military considerations and not for their innate beauty. Some new purchasers were able to adapt a former monastery with great ingenuity, creating from a house shut away from the world a mansion which often came to be the focal point of its community. These are essential elements which point to the 16th century as the period when the country house in its generally accepted sense was born. There had been manor houses and parks for centuries; substantial houses occupied by substantial families which still survive because their owners never wished to rebuild or alter. Houses in the country they still remain, but their function is essentially different.

The country house was more than a home; indeed, there are still those who remember them not as home at all, but as uncomfortable, draughty, ill-lit and rambling houses where their families happened to live. They were, in a sense, family headquarters, bases of social and political power, and as such they had to be obvious expressions of wealth and influence. Patrons of seats in Parliament and owners of wide acres had to be patrons of the Arts, declaring their influence by their taste and their taste by their choice of architect or designer. But behind the glamour was another world, a community which served and supported, which provided labour in kitchen and scullery, in garden and greenhouse and stable; a vast army of people who

Window in Mellifont Abbey, Wookey, probably from the bishops' manor house at Court Farm.

Sharpham Park, Walton. The arms of Glastonbury Abbey, the pelican of Abbot Bere and the portcullis of Henry VII.

Court Farm, Wookey, incorporates an arch from Bishop Jocelin's manor house, perhaps the entrance to the chapel, within the buttressed wing.

tenanted the farms, who scurried up and down service stairs and feasted in servants' halls.

There have always been families and individuals who have seen the country as a welcome retreat from the pressures of politics or business; there have been others who have preferred the rigours of the London scene. For Sir William Wyndham or the Elder Pitt the Somerset countryside was a solace in the presence of political failure. While Orchard Wyndham became for a time a focal point of dissident Tory politicians, Burton Pynsent was simply a welcome haven where the uncertain landscape of Europe could be safely exchanged for the realism of Pitt's own creation. Hinton was hardly exciting enough for the first Baron Poulett after his experience at the Stuart Court, but the first Earl Poulett probably brought Queen Anne there and later generations convinced themselves that the great Palladian south wing had been built especially for her.

And there was the great influence of the country house. Ven was the power base from which generations of Medlycotts ensured their membership of the House of Commons. Dunster, without causing undue scandal, managed to influence the results of democracy at Minehead for the benefit of the Luttrells, and Halswell exercised some influence for the Egmonts at Bridgwater. And it is inconceivable that conversations at Newton Park and Ston Easton did not on occasion concern and probably influence the politics of Bath and Bristol.

Other families had more modest aims, farming more modest estates, husbanding their resources until fashion inspired them to rebuild or extend. The last hundred years have been less kind to the country house, although various forms of corporate ownership have at worst preserved the essential fabric and at best, through private generosity, have rescued from demolition and then in various ways splendidly restored. The balls and weekend parties may have gone, but many Somerset houses are accessible as never before.

Barrington Court

Top. The south front of the Elizabethan house.

Bottom. The north front from beyond the forecourt, with the stable block of 1674 just visible to the west.

From the time when Colonel A.A. Lyle took a lease from the National Trust of what was part farmhouse, part cider cellar, part virtual ruin, and recreated it as a home for the extensive collection of fine woodwork he had rescued from destruction, the history of this important house has often been told. There was not, to begin with, unanimous agreement about the date of the building. J.E. Forbes, the architect responsible for the restoration between 1920 and 1925, actually thought it belonged to two phases, a shell of about 1518 when the then owners came into money through a satisfactory marriage alliance, to which a central porch was added about 1570. It was, in effect, a skilfull combination of late Gothic and Elizabethan in style. A young and enthusiastic Christopher Hussey rejected the Elizabethan interpretation in favour of a 'final and most free expression of pure Gothic design' with French influence, but he admitted that the porch was added and dated it to the 1530s. It was this view which generally held the field, giving rise to phrases such as 'exceptional historical interest' for a house of this date so far from the sophistication of the London scene.

So according to this interpretation Barrington was built after the marriage of Henry, son and heir of Giles, Baron Daubeney, to the daughter of George Neville, Baron Abergavenny. The young husband was thus wealthy enough to build a new mansion. The fact that his father had served as Henry VII's ambassador to the French Court helped to explain a certain French flavour in the twisted finials. But there is no evidence that the Daubeneys had need for an injection of cash. Sir Giles Daubeney, great-grandfather of Henry, died in 1446 at his home at Barrington leaving large quantities of plate and estates in Lincolnshire and Bedfordshire as well as in Somerset. His house, which stood north-east of the present building where traces of a moat may still be seen, was by the later 14th century very substantial, comprising a hall with two-storeyed solar, another storeyed wing, two kitchens, a chapel and a gatehouse. Giles Daubeney, Henry's father, had been a loyal servant to Edward IV, was exiled under Richard III but returned with Henry Tudor, whom he served loyally as diplomat, military commander and courtier. He was buried in Westminster Abbey in 1508, leaving his son and heir a teenager.

That young man followed his father at Court, but the new king reaped with flamboyance where his father had sown with frugality, and the new courtier shared his sovereign's tastes. He received New

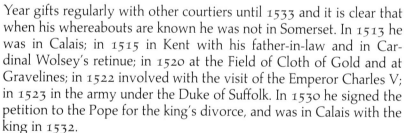

Year gifts regularly with other courtiers until 1533 and it is clear that when his whereabouts are known he was not in Somerset. In 1513 he was in Calais; in 1515 in Kent with his father-in-law and in Cardinal Wolsey's retinue; in 1520 at the Field of Cloth of Gold and at Gravelines; in 1522 involved with the visit of the Emperor Charles V; in 1523 in the army under the Duke of Suffolk. In 1530 he signed the petition to the Pope for the king's divorce, and was in Calais with the king in 1532.

All this does not prove that he did not build Barrington Court as J.E. Forbes claimed, but it is clear that from the 1520s Henry Daubeney was in serious financial difficulties and was even deeper in debt after spending large sums to acquire an earldom. But for what purpose? By two wives, the second a Howard, he had no heir. Henry was the last of his line and yet he was determined on a more prestigious title. His efforts were rewarded when he became the first and last Earl of Bridgwater (Harry Bridgwater he signed himself) at a cost which included wages for eighty horsemen and new liveries in the colours of the Lord Privy Seal (Thomas Cromwell) for a parade along Cheapside. But when he died in 1548 he seems to have possessed only one residence, South Perrott in Dorset, where he had been

Above left. The staircase in the restored east wing.

Opposite. The 17th-century stables, converted into a house between 1920 and 1925, with gardens designed by Gertrude Jekyll.

living for the last thirteen years. The estate of Barrington was still his for life but, according to the lawyers, it was only a 'lordship, manor and park'.

For several years Barrington passed from creditor to Crown and then in 1552 from Henry, Duke of Suffolk, to William Clifton, a prosperous London merchant. It was evidently at first an investment, but by 1559 Clifton had left London for Somerset and was at Barrington when he died in 1564.

Clifton was a nouveau-riche who originated in Norwich as a property-owner, made his way in the customs and property speculation in London, in company with Sir Thomas Tresham, and bought his first Somerset property in 1546. He or his son Sir John Clifton (d. 1593) must surely be accounted at least builders of the central porch, very like a dated example at Kirby Hall, Northamptonshire. And if that is agreed, then one or the other must surely be accounted the builder of the rest of the house, for masons' marks lightly incised in the golden freestone of the porch are repeated through the remainder of the building, visible only by a trick of the light. The East Anglian Cliftons had only to look to Kentwell Hall, Hengrave or Channons to find models for their new house in the West Country. One further piece of evidence has now disappeared, but until about 1920 there was a porch at the west end of Barrington bearing a coat of arms probably used by William Clifton.

Daubeney or Clifton, the mellow Ham stone ashlar house is built in the shape of an E, the main range containing the hall with probable parlour and solar, now the staircase, to the east; and to the west a buttery beyond the screens passage. The porch is placed in the centre of the south front and two long wings project forward to form a forecourt, one containing the original kitchen. Staircases formerly occupied the angles between the wings and the main range. The front rises to three storeys, the porch to four, and a long gallery stretches the length of the house immediately under the roof.

Although not strictly symmetrical, since the hall has two lights and the buttery one, the south front has seven gables, four created from the gallery dormers, decorated with octagonal buttresses and finished with three twisted finials with ogee scale-work caps and traditional English crockets. This skyline, restored through the generosity of Sir Ian Lyle in 1968, is spectacular and faces across lawns, a cricket pitch and wide green park.

William Clifton's grandson Gervase, Lord Clifton, sold Barrington in 1605 to his brother-in-law Sir Thomas Phelips of Montacute. William Strode bought it in 1625 after it had been mortgaged twice and his family retained it, despite a seriously faulted title, until the middle of the 18th century when it had become little more than a farmhouse. The Strodes, however, left their mark by building a large brick quadrangular stable block to the west of the main house in 1674, with room for twelve houses, two coaches, a granary and a brewhouse. The Strodes were also responsible for two early-17th-century overmantels on the first floor of the house, the one in plaster showing the Judgement of Solomon, the other in Ham stone with the arms of William Strode and of his wife Joan Barnard of Downside, to whom he owed much of his fortune.

By the 19th century the property, including some 200 acres of land, was known as Court Farm. It passed to the National Trust through the generosity of Miss J.L. Woodward of Clevedon, and after its restoration the Lyle family occupied the former stables as a dwelling. The original house was reconstructed and redecorated, incorporating Colonel Lyle's collection of panelling and wainscot and a screen from King's Lynn. The Lyles also formed the gardens to the west according to designs by Gertrude Jekyll, and added farm buildings and cottages to the north and north-west to form a 'manor place' inspired by the Arts and Crafts movement.

The Lyles have now left Barrington but the house, open to the public on Wednesday afternoons from April to September, is sub-let to Stuart Interiors whose antiques and quality reproduction furniture are so effectively displayed in sympathetic surroundings. It is a setting which owes its existence to the generosity of a knowledgeable collector and a talented architect.

The early 17th-century Ham stone overmantel in the first-floor parlour bearing the arms of William Strode and Joan Barnard.

Brympton D'Evercy

The judgement of Christopher Hussey that Brympton is the 'exquisite summary of English country life' will surely not be challenged by anyone who comes upon the family home of the Clive-Ponsonby-Fanes. And if three noble names in one sound a trifle formidable, their owners are certainly not; only their responsibility for a noble demesne. Between them, Fanes, Ponsonbys and Clives have been here for only two-and-a-half centuries, half the lifetime of their home. Such is fame that the d'Evercys — from Evrecy near Caen in Normandy — were here for only a century beginning in Henry III's reign and yet endowed the estate with their name.

Sir Peter d'Evercy, who represented Somerset twice in Parliament under Edward II, died in 1325 leaving behind in his hamlet of Brympton a 'capital messuage with gardens and closes adjoining' worth five shillings a year — a formal and unrealistic valuation quite normal at the time — a home farm of 105 acres, mostly under plough, three freehold tenant farms, and seventeen small-holders. Sir Peter also left an only daughter Amice, wife of John de Glamorgan, and a widow who was evidently in actual possession of the house and outlived her son-in-law. Peter de Glamorgan, son of Amice, did not long survive and when he died in 1343 an enquiry on behalf of the Crown and the heir referred to a manor house 'sufficiently built' and 'a certain garden adjoining, planted with divers and many apple trees', the whole covering some two acres. And after that were listed three open fields north, east and west of the house, one sown with Winter corn, one with Spring corn, and one left fallow; some meadow in the valley bottom by the stream; and a piece of land once pasture and now planted with oak trees. And after the fields in the enquiry return came a list of tenant farmers and cottagers, forty households in all, some with only fifteen acres and charged to work for their lord and serve as village blacksmith, drover or domestic servant.

For a century or so the successive owners of the manor can be traced clearly enough, but of the house there is no clue, 'sufficiently' built or not. Inheritance and purchase brought the estate to the ubiquitous Sydenham family at the time of the Wars of the Roses. John Sydenham seems to have acquired it with the hand of Joan, daughter of John Stourton of nearby Preston. Their son Walter died in 1469, only a year after his father. He did not mention the house in his will but requested burial in the newly-built north aisle of

Detail of the tomb of Sir John Sydenham (died 1636) in Brympton church.

the little church hard by, surely a sign that the house was indeed his home.

That 'new' building may just be a clue to the beginnings of the house as it stands today, the product of this new branch of the Sydenhams who stayed here for more than two hundred years. It may well have been begun by the first John Sydenham, and perhaps identifiable as his work is the now detached building between the mansion and the churchyard, known as the Priest House but earlier called Chantry House, Dower House or even 'horticultural appendage'. None of these names seem to fit a range which contains a first-floor hall and chamber with a fine roof of collar beams and cusped windbraces over rooms which later were used as stables. The wing might, however, have formed part of the medieval house of which not much else now remains. Hinton and Orchard Wyndham both had at least one wing coming forward from the hall range; Fairfield still has such a wing, complete with first-floor hall. Might the house at Brympton have once stood on two if not three sides of a forecourt, its entrance facade having a pair of turrets flanking the porch entrance to a great hall? One turret still survives, no longer in its proper corner position; and the hall windows, perhaps of the early 16th century like the chambers and parlour beyond the turret, are embedded in the south-west corner of the present building. The remodelling of Brympton, datable by the elaborate carvings and the arms of Henry VIII to show that the Sydenhams had a connexion with the Royal House, could well have been the work of John Sydenham II (d. 1543).

Still it was not a large house: a main range with hall and parlours, a front wing with a second hall on the first floor, and a rear range, probably forming one or two sides of a rear courtyard and including kitchens and other necessary offices. It was left to another John Sydenham (for seven generations the eldest son was always John) to transform the old house into a fashionable mansion. But which John, and when?

The Tudor west front with the so-called Priest House on the right and the charming clock tower over the former porch on the left.

The prospect of the manor place at
Brympton in Kip's engraving of the early
18th century.

The great south front of Brympton, ten bays long under a
balustrade and a hipped roof, with windows alternately under trian-
gular and segmental pediments, has been, like the similar wings at
Hinton and Ashton Court, attributed wrongly to Inigo Jones. It is
much more likely that all three are the work of one family of masons
using designs from Serlio's *Book of Architecture*, published in 1619 and
the main source of inspiration for English Palladianism. And there
were obvious links between all three houses: Thomas Smythe of
Long Ashton and John Posthumous Sydenham of Brympton (so
named because he was born in 1642 after the death of his father) had
married Poulett ladies from Hinton, the one a daughter, the other
a grand daughter of John, the first Baron Poulett. Stylistically
Brympton is more sophisticated and regular than Hinton, whose
form was governed by the rooms in the range it was replacing. Every
historian of Brympton has found himself quoting a description of the
house in 1697 as 'a very large new built mansion house' which, it was
then claimed, had cost either £16,000 or £20,000. If 'new built' is
taken literally, then the builder must be Sir John Posthumous Sydenham. A leaden rainwater head on the great south front bears the arms
of himself and his first wife, Elizabeth Poulett. They were married in
1664 and she died in 1669. The work thus seems to belong to, or at
least to have been finished in, the early years of the Restoration. Yet
it is at least possible that the work had been begun in the late 1630s
after Long Ashton (c. 1633-4) and Hinton (1636) had been completed, for did not Sir John Sydenham raise over £48,000 before his
death in 1642, possibly in part to cover his building enterprises, a
task brought to an end either by his own death or by the uncertainty
of the times?

Whenever the south front was built, the Sydenhams in the person of Sir Philip, heir of Sir John Posthumous, were deep in financial trouble by the 1690s, a disease which also afflicted Sir Philip's
creditor and successor there, Thomas Penny. Penny died in 1730 and
his trustees mortgaged the house and estate to Francis Fane of Bris-

tol, M.P. and a commissioner of Trade and Plantations 1746-56.
From him it passed in 1757 to his brother Thomas, attorney at law,
long-serving Clerk of the Society of Merchant Venturers of Bristol, and Whig M.P. for Lyme, where he was patron of both seats.
This evidently prosperous man, whose wife was daughter of a Bristol merchant and widow of a London Chancery Clerk, was great-
grandson of Sir Francis Fane, Royalist commander in the Civil War
and dramatist and poet in Charles II's reign, and the youngest son
of Francis, the first Fane Earl of Westmorland. By an extraordinary
failure of heirs in the senior branch of the family, Thomas Fane M.P.,
owner of Brympton, found himself in 1762 no longer eligible to sit in
the House of Commons, for he had become by the death of his
second cousin once removed the eighth Earl of Westmorland.

The entrance hall early in the 20th
century.

It was not, presumably, a complete surprise, for the seventh earl
was well over 70 at his death. And as if in preparation Thomas's heir
married into two ducal families, although he was buried with the rest
of his father's more modest line at Westbury on Trym outside Bristol.
Brympton was for many years the home of Jane, second wife of the
tenth earl, from whom she was for so long estranged. A charming
but restless lady, she was described by Henry Fox as 'perhaps not
mad, but no body ever approached so near it with so much reason'.
Her removal to Brympton in company with her remarkable daughter
Lady Georgiana Fane, the great friend of the Duke of Wellington,
brought life to a house which the Fanes had hitherto somewhat
neglected.

Indeed, little had been altered since the late 17th century when the
State Rooms in the south wing were wainscotted. Thomas Penny
built the present, rather fantastic porch, originally as an oriel, removing the earlier porch to the north side of the forecourt garden where
it forms the base of a charming clock tower. The Fanes put in the
Georgian fireplaces in the State Rooms, and Lady Georgiana trans-

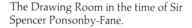

The Drawing Room in the time of Sir
Spencer Ponsonby-Fane.

formed the gardens. In the early 18th century, according to an
engraving by Kip, the house was surrounded by formally planted
orchards to the north and east, and a grassy courtyard to the west
separating the house from the stables. To the south lay a terrace and
formal lawns, a tree-lined avenue, parterres and canals. South of the
churchyard was the vegetable garden with fish pond and another
canal. Lady Georgiana rebuilt the terrace and seems to have created
the garden as it is today, the large lake in place of the parterre
mirroring the south front in its waters.

At her death in 1874 she left Brympton to her nephew and godson
Spencer Ponsonby, an inheritance heavily encumbered with debt. A
younger son of the fifth Earl of Bessborough, Spencer had already
made his name as a diplomat and private secretary to successive
Foreign Ministers. In 1857 he had begun a distinguished career in the
Royal Household as Comptroller in the Lord Chamberlain's Department and Gentleman Usher to Queen Victoria. Another claim to
fame was his passion for cricket and he was co-founder of the famous

The 17th-century south front from across the lake.

amateur team called I Zingari (the Gypsies) who regularly played at Brympton.

On inheriting the estate, Spencer Ponsonby by Royal Licence took the Fane family name to add to his own, a fine gesture to his predecessors at Brympton. The tradition was maintained two generations later when Violet Ponsonby-Fane, who lived in the house in the absence of her brother in Japan, married Captain Edward Clive. In 1937 their son Nicholas inherited Brympton from his uncle and assumed his names, creating that formidable combination. Charles Clive-Ponsonby-Fane bravely returned to the house with his young wife after it had for some years been occupied as a school. Between them they have restored Brympton to something of its former splendour and have tamed the wilderness his remarkable grandmother had created. His own interests include the garden and vines flourish on the slopes overlooking the forecourt. The apple trees of Brympton in the 14th century have their modern successors.

Burton Pynsent

The year 1804 might have seen the end of a generous gesture and a magnificent concept. The prospective purchaser of the Burton Pynsent estate was given the option of buying the materials of the mansion and the column which stood across the valley in the distance, and allowed free access to pull down the house and fell the timber for a period of three years. So might all traces of a great enterprise have been wiped from the face of the earth. In the event, the mansion was reduced to reasonable proportions and the column was saved.

The mansion had been enormous: a 'considerable part' was a 'modern brick structure', the remainder 'ancient Gothic'. There was a ballroom measuring 60ft by 27ft, a drawing room 30ft by 28ft, a dining room 34ft by 21ft, a library 36ft by 19ft, a bird room 24ft by 20ft. The building rambled on with several waiting and passage rooms, a morning sitting room, a second drawing room, and a grotto room. Two stone staircases led to twenty chambers and dressing rooms, and there was a detached servants' hall and kitchen. Nearby stood a mews with five coach houses, and four stables for twenty-five horses.

The 'ancient Gothic' part of the mansion probably dated back to the 16th century when the Jennings family established themselves at Burton, and it was this house which passed by descent and marriage to Sir William Pynsent, a Whig gentleman of eccentric behaviour who, according to Horace Walpole, 'was said to have had not many scruples, living to her death with his only daughter in pretty notorious incest'. What had been added to the Elizabethan house can only be guessed at, for what survives is a brick wing of modest proportions which had been built, possibly to his own designs, by William Pitt, Earl of Chatham.

The change of ownership from Pynsent to Pitt is a curious story. Sir William acquired Burton through his marriage to Mary, daughter and co-heiress of Thomas Jennings. He survived his wife and all his children, the last of whom died in 1763. There was a nephew, 'a very quarrelsome mortal', according to Sir William's lawyer, a niece and three grand nephews; and in his will, drawn up in October 1764, he left them 1,000 guineas each. He made several small bequests to servants in the form of annuities, but all his real estate, both in Somerset and in Wiltshire, he left to William Pitt of Hayes, Kent, 'late Secretary of State', whom he also appointed his sole executor.

William Pitt, 1st Earl of Chatham (1708-1778), owner of Burton from 1765 until his death in 1778 and creator of the landscaped grounds.

The east front of William Pitt's addition of 1766-7.

It is something of a mystery why Pynsent should have left his wealth to Pitt. It was said at the time that Pynsent admired Pitt's patriotism; and it was later suggested that Pitt's opposition to a tax on cider had been a deciding factor. There was even a splendid tale that Pynsent had called upon Pitt to acquaint him with his design and had been dismissed by Pitt's servants because of his shabby appearance. Pynsent himself makes no mention of his motive in the will, hoping only that Pitt 'will like my Burton estate where I now live well enough to make it his country seat'.

Pitt was still out of office when Pynsent died early in January 1765, and he seems to have lost little time in coming down to Somerset and in commemorating his benefactor. A column was what he had in mind, something like the pillar at Stowe designed by James Gibbs which had cost £830, and he evidently approached Lancelot (Capability) Brown for a design. 'If there are any parts you disapprove of', Brown wrote, 'we can very easy correct them when I shall have the Honor of seeing you. The figure I have put on the Pedestal

is that of Gratitude, conveying to posterity the name of Pinsant, which indeed he himself has distinguished and without flattery done in the most effectual manner by making you his heir'.

There were problems about the column, but work on a new wing for the house was under way by October. This wing, now the main part of the present house, was probably designed and executed by the Bath master mason John Ford the Elder (1711-67). 'I advance apace in bricks and mortar', Pitt told his brother-in-law Earl Temple, 'but the monumental column must wait the return of spring'. As winter approached, Pitt's gout was particularly troublesome and he proposed 'carrying my legs, since they will not carry me, to Bath towards the end of November, if I hold out so long, and try once again to prop a shattered tenement with the help of steel waters'.

In February 1766 the bricklayers were unable to work on the house because of the hard frost, but the carpenters were there, and Philip Pear, the Curry Rivel builder, reported to Pitt that he had opened a quarry in the barley field and had begun to dig for the foundations of the column on Troy Hill, across the valley from the house. He discovered that rock was to be found only at a depth of 17ft, and therefore awaited further orders. In September 1766 John Ford was paid £300 on account, 'which he received with great thankfulness'. A year later Pear sent in an account for over £337 from masons, plumbers and lime burners. By then the column was finished, and Brown wrote to Lady Chatham wanting 'above all things to know . . . how the Pillar pleases his Lordship'.

But Pitt's pastoral idyll was for the moment over. In July 1766 he was back in the government as Lord Privy Seal, and while his health permitted was its virtual head under the nominal leadership of the Duke of Grafton. He resigned as M.P. for Bath and was created Viscount Pitt of Burton Pynsent and Earl of Chatham, much to the distress of some of his friends. 'My Lord Chatham', declared his enemies, 'has nothing like the influence which Mr Pitt enjoyed. You see the effects of Somersetshire: it has metamorphosed a bawling orator into an old Apple woman'. He was ill again early in 1767 and he evidently retired to the country, where he began the transformation of the landscape, inspired by the work of his friend Lancelot Brown at Stowe but designed entirely by himself. Near the house the formal gardens were almost instantly created, with seats and Chinese railings installed by Mr Pear; further away there were grander designs for a more long-term creation. Captain Samuel Hood sent seeds and plants of birch, black spruce, ash, maple and buckthorn from Nova Scotia; Macaulay described how relays of labourers worked at Burton even by torchlight planting cedars sent down in great numbers from London. Earl Temple complimented Pitt on 'the rising towers and I hope flourishing plantations which your active mind has plann'd and expeditious right hand already executed — so far breaking in upon Mr Brown's department by adorning the country which you were not permitted to save'.

So cedars, limes and elms were planted around lawns and in avenues, all artfully arranged to lead the eye and the stroller from the house and its immediate surroundings to the monument on Troy Hill. An arch and a pump provided points of interest, and plantations, woody hangings and a wilderness were created. Farming, hunting and planting became Pitt's chief delight, and his family shared his enthusiasm. His wife had long ago declared her love of the place because it was their own and because 'there is something not quite common about it'. Young William Pitt and his elder brother spent much of their childhood there; William, at the age of 13, wrote a tragedy entitled 'Laurentius, King of Clarum' which was performed in the house. He remembered Burton fondly and when Prime Minister in 1783 declared that he preferred the view of Sedgemoor and Troy Hill to the more famous grounds of Stowe. Nearly ten years later he apologised to Lord Grenville for not being able to show him Burton in person.

By that time Lady Chatham was living there alone, for her husband had collapsed in the House of Lords in May 1778 and had died a few days later. Hester Temple, sister of Earl Temple of Stowe and from 1761 Baroness Chatham in her own right, 'possessed grace, virtue, and good sense in abundance, and the marriage [had] proved to be one of unalloyed happiness and mutual affection'. She remained at Burton until her death in April 1803, where for her last three years she had enjoyed the company of her granddaughter Lady Hester Stanhope. Her death brought disaster on the house and the estate. The family rescued the memorial urn erected on the south side of the house by Lady Chatham in 1781 to the design of Mr Bacon; and the family's physician, Dr Woodforde of Taunton, purchased the column on Troy Hill. But the speculator who bought the rest of the estate in 1805 for £8,810 pulled down most of the house, and the grounds created with such care and imagination were neglected.

William Pitt the Younger (1759-1806), who lived at Burton as a child and declared he loved the view of Sedgemoor and Troy Hill better than the grounds of Stowe.

The memorial column to Sir William Pynsent c.1766, designed by 'Capability' Brown for William Pitt, 1st Earl of Chatham.

The Pinneys, later owners of the estate, repaired the column in 1905 just before selling to Mrs Crossley. She added the gabled entrance front to the house and restored Pitt's modest addition of three inter-communicating rooms, one of which has been identified as the bird room of the great mansion, so called because it was decorated with four landscapes by Bogdani featuring birds, fowls and rabbits. Mrs Crossley also restored the garden. Across the valley, the column has fared less well, although the present owner of Burton, Mr John Schroder, is making great efforts to prevent further deterioration. The Burton Monument, which cost Pitt some £2,000 to build, now needs expensive repair. The Portland stone ashlar facing is coming away from the core; the finial, urn and dome need to be rebuilt. The final cost may be in the order of five times the original cost of erection.

Coker Court

When John de Mandeville died in 1276 he was the fifth generation to be lord of the manor of East Coker. He died deranged, but legally in possession here of a house, a garden, dovehouses, and a vineyard worth 20s. a year; a home farm and, in the park outside the wood, 105 acres of pasture. With the lordship went the right to appoint a parson to the church. A few years later John's son, also John, was described as holding both East and West Coker of the heir of the Earl of Vernon, of the manor of Christchurch Twineham, and that heir held of the King in chief. All this feudal formality was important because Robert de Mandeville, grandson of the first John, was outlawed for felony in 1305-6 and the income from his manor passed to the Crown for a year and a day and the feudal lord thereafter took possession.

In this way the Mandeville family gave place to the heir of the Earl of Vernon, namely Hugh Courtenay, later first Earl of Devon. Hugh's interests were principally in Devon, where he owned the great feudal honor of Okehampton. Hugh died in 1340 and was followed by his son, also Hugh, who married Margaret de Bohun, granddaughter of Edward I. She held East Coker as part of her dower after her husband's death in 1377; and then after her own in 1391 it passed to her seventh son, Sir Peter Courtenay, one of the most flamboyant men of his generation. On his death in 1405 caused, it was said, by a wound received at a joust, the manor passed, according to the settlement arranged by his father, to his brother Sir Philip Courtenay of Powderham in Devon. On Philip's death in 1406 it went to his son Richard, a priest and Bishop of Norwich 1413-15. Richard's nephew Philip succeeded and held the manor until his death in 1463, although it is evident that for at least eight years before that his son William had been resident in Somerset, probably in East Coker. Philip, meanwhile, continued his doubtfully legal shipping activities from Dartmouth and managed to escape the fatal consequences of political involvement to which the senior branch of his family was for several generations prone.

The few surviving account rolls for the manor in the 15th century can hardly be expected to reveal the date of the earliest part of the present house: historians rarely have that good fortune. But the hall range, the north side of the present house, is thought to belong to the mid 15th century, presumably the time of Sir Philip Courtenay (1415-63) or of his son Sir William (1463-85).

The range now comprises a two-storeyed porch, screens passage with arches marking entrances to the former pantry, kitchen and buttery, and a hall with an oriel chamber balancing the porch. The hall and oriel chamber have large, two-light transomed windows, their tops decorated with trefoiled ogees. The hall roof is of arched braces with a trefoil in each spandrel, and windbraces. Beyond the oriel chamber stood the dais and solar. Hall, solar, and service range were surely in place when in 1471-2 Sir William Courtenay's bailiff recorded his expenses when the young masters William and Edward came from Muchelney, when he himself rode to the Duke of Clarence at Christmas, and when he made two particular payments: 16d 'for glazing of the stair window' and 2s 6d to the tiler for pointing the east side of Sir William's chamber. Here is proof enough of the solar range beyond the hall. In 1474-5 the bailiff spent 33s 4d 'for the great garden and a close under the court' and recorded an income of £5 6s 8d from the park. This park, according to later accounts, seems to have grown in importance: in 1509-10 6s 6d was spent on a bridge and a way leading to it; in the next year the way to the park was repaired and in 1516-17 13d was charged for making a hedge and 'le Spryngett' (spring gate) there.

Sir William Courtenay, MP for Somerset 1455-6, was living at Coker in 1458 when he received a pardon, presumably for his Yorkist sympathies. Ten years later he had moved to Devon and, at least loyal to Clarence, presumably his patron, sided first with one party and then with another in the political crisis of 1470-1. Finally loyal to Richard III he probably died before Bosworth. The family retained possession of East Coker until 1591 when another Sir William Courtenay sold the capital messuage and woods called East Coker park. A year or two later house and park came into the possession of the Phelipses of Montacute who in 1616 sold to Dr William Helyar. Helyar's descendants lived in the house until 1950.

Dr Helyar, like the Courtenays, came from Devon. By the time he bought the manor he was already a canon of Exeter cathedral and archdeacon of Barnstaple, his canonry given by the Crown at the request of Sir Walter Raleigh in 1602. By the time he came to Somerset Helyar was already 57 years old, quite elderly for the time; and yet he lived on until 1645, a stout defender of the Church of England as by law established and by Laud embellished. He so stoutly defended the cathedral at Exeter against fanatical Independents that he was dragged from his bed, beaten, pelted with mud and confined to a prison hulk until a fine of £800 was paid. Parliament then graciously offered him its protection in consideration of a further £200 which was described as a loan. The archdeacon died at Coker, unrepentantly Royalist, at the age of 86.

According to his neighbour Thomas Gerard of Trent, Archdeacon Helyar 'not only well repaired the old buildings, but also added new unto them'. One significant alteration which still survives is the fine stone screen in the hall, its double entrances flanked by paired Doric

Above. The medieval Great Hall with Archdeacon Helyar's fireplace.

Right. The Great Hall showing the timber roof and the 17th-century stone screen.

Opposite top. The north entrance front, with the fine transomed windows of the Great Hall and Oriel Chamber.

Opposite below. The 18th-century east front.

columns. The screen was once topped with a balustrade bearing the arms of the Courtenays and the Phelipses as well as his own. He also added the hall fireplace, also with Doric columns, and at least one other fireplace, decorated with heavy strapwork. Beyond the Helyars' panelled dining room is another with a plaster ceiling which bears the Helyar arms and probably dates from his time. The Laudian archdeacon was also a typical country squire anxious to follow the fashion of his times.

Helyar's grandson and heir, another William, was as strong for the King as his grandfather had been. He raised a troop of horse but was obliged to surrender to Fairfax in 1643 and was again the loser at Exeter in 1646. His lands were taken until he paid the huge fine of £1522 in 1648, but he lived to find power and prosperity again. He served as sheriff of Somerset in 1661-2 and survived until 1697 leaving to his son and heir William his house called Coker Court and estates including his lease of a sugar plantation in Jamaica, complete with negroes and distilling equipment. The Jamaican property was charged with £600 to support the almshouses below the Court which his grandfather had founded.

William succeeded William six times between the archdeacon's day and 1820, and it is to that William who succeeded in 1742 and who died in 1783 that the major changes in the house are due. Those changes are traced in two account books now among the Helyar archives at the Somerset Record Office which record building carried out between May 1766 and February 1770 under the general direction of Joseph Dixon, a mason and surveyor of St Alban's Street, London. A family tradition that the work was designed by the royal architect Sir William Chambers may well be true, but only in the sense that Chambers' *Treatise on Civil Architecture* was by that time well known to such men as Dixon, and the new work certainly bears all the characteristics of the restrained style Chambers favoured.

The account books record the expenditure of over £3700, by no means the total cost of the undertaking. Materials came from a wide area: lime from Mells in the Mendips for burning on site; slate from Load Bridge where it had come by water probably from Cornwall; stone tile from Ham Hill; stone and slate from Weymouth. Brick was made on the estate at a new kiln. The accounts, partly kept by Robert Friend as clerk of works and partly as a weekly wage book, indicate the progress of the work, beginning with radical alterations to the great hall and continuing first with alterations to, followed by demolition of, what were described as the 'old building' and the 'old partments'. The latest works were a kitchen, stables, scullery and water closet.

In sum, Dixon's work was a new east range beginning at the east end of the hall and running south and then west, providing a new suite of elegant rooms replacing the old solar wing of the medieval house. The plain east front faces a terraced garden and has seven bays with a central three-bay pediment. A Venetian window at its north end replaced a light in the solar end of the hall; another, described in the accounts as Palladian, overlooks the court-yard and lights the plain stair. Interior decoration is more elaborate; the fireplace in the central room on the ground floor has a fine overmantel with fluted Corinthian columns and a broken pediment. On the first floor there were two rooms decorated with contemporary Chinese themes, a particular interest of Chambers. The accounts are silent about the paper but record 24½ lbs of 'flower' for hanging it.

Less acceptable to modern tastes, and certainly to those of later owners, was the treatment of the great hall. A floor was inserted to provide rooms on a new first floor whose safety could only be guaranteed by the support of two pillars. The rooms thus created had plaster ceilings and the roof was pierced with dormer windows. One wall was pierced to make a window for a gallery.

The medieval hall was restored to much of its original splendour and the west side of the house rebuilt for servants' rooms and offices in 1900 by the last of the Helyars, Dorothy, daughter of Horace Helyar and wife of Major Godfrey Walker-Heneage, D.S.O., M.V.O., Grenadier Guards. All the building work was done by the estate workmen to the highest standards, and included the removal of paint from the Ham stone screen and chimney piece in the hall.

Mrs Walker-Heneage, a highly respected figure in East Coker, died in 1947 and her son David only three years later. The sale of the contents of the house, conducted in the tapestry-hung great hall, is a vivid memory of the writer. For several years the house was used as a preparatory school and suffered some of the consequences, but more recently it has returned to domestic use and is now divided. The hall and the east and south ranges have been restored by a knowledge-able owner who appreciates both the quality of the interior and the importance of the setting.

Court, church and almshouses, approached up a drive under a canopy of trees, will be for many the most memorable glimpse of England: manor-house and church in close proximity, evidence of the ancient tie of spiritual and temporal. And in the church are the ashes of a poet whose ancestors had left Coker for New England in the 17th century. T. S. Eliot's deep feelings for the past will be echoed there by many who come from all over the world to pay homage to his memory and see as they walk under the trees the house which was already old when Andrew Elliott was baptised in the parish church of East Coker in 1627.

The Helyar Almshouses, founded by Archdeacon Helyar (died 1645).

Court House

The name Luttrell is for many synonymous either with Dunster or with the famous psalter, but while there is justice in both statements, the greater justice would be their connection with this much more modest house. Today a Union Flag with a special device at its centre often flies above it, signifying that Her Majesty's Lord-Lieutenant of Somerset, Colonel Geoffrey Walter Fownes Luttrell, is at home; successor here to his forbear Geoffrey Luttrell, who himself just outlived King John. The first Geoffrey did not actually own East Quantoxhead, but his marriage to the delightfully-named Frethesant, great grand-daughter of Ralph Pagnell, the Domesday lord, brought the estate in 1232 to Geoffrey's son Andrew. So the manor has changed hands by marriage and descent but never by sale from the 11th century to the present, and Luttrells have been there, with interruptions usually of their own choosing, from the reign of Henry III to the present. The psalter, its decoration a brilliant evocation of contemporary life, was made in the early 14th century for another Geoffrey Luttrell, lord of Irnham in Lincolnshire, descendant of the Andrew who had first acquired Quantoxhead.

All this sounds rather complicated, and it must also be added that until the 1230s the Luttrells, like the Pagnells, did not belong to the West Country, but were more closely associated with properties in the East and North including land now occupied by a motorway service station – Newport Pagnell. Andrew Luttrell gave Quantoxhead to his second son Alexander who, in theory in days of paper-feudalism, held his manor as of his senior cousins of Irnham. But it was a purely nominal arrangement: Alexander, when he died in 1273, was as much lord of the place as his father and grandfather had been before him. And at his death a jury declared that at the heart of his estate was the manor house with a stone-roofed building opposite the hall and another elsewhere, a gatehouse, farm buildings, gardens and fishponds. The jury might also have mentioned the church, had that been their business, to complete the picture which can still be enjoyed today, a scene (complete with ducks on the millpond) which for many is the epitome of England.

In the 13th and 14th centuries the Luttrells were a family of modest means and modest achievements. Alexander probably died in the Holy Land where he had gone in the retinue of Prince Edward, soon to be Edward I. Andrew, Alexander's son, was summoned from his then home in Devon to fight the Scots in 1301; Andrew's son

Alexander became a knight at Edward III's coronation in 1327 and his grandson John was made one of the first knights of the Order of the Bath at Henry IV's coronation in 1399. After serving as sheriff of Somerset and Dorset in 1401 he supported the King two years later when Percies, Mortimers, Glendower and others rose in rebellion against the Crown.

The church and Court House from the south-east, showing part of the magnificent garden.

With the death of Sir John in 1403 the direct line of Luttrells at East Quantoxhead came to an end, although one of his illegitimate children survived to serve the family at Dunster where Sir John's heir, his cousin Hugh, began to concentrate the family's interests. But the old manor and estate were not neglected. Records from Hugh's time onwards give fascinating but frustrating glimpses into the house when craftsmen were paid for work there. A 'great chamber' is mentioned in the account roll for the financial year 1403-4; in that for 1408-9 a carpenter was paid for making a 'stresschold' (is that a threshold ?) for the oriel door and a new 'enterclose' for the oriel itself; and in 1421-2 there is mention of a tiled 'loigge'. So this was no plain and ordinary house even if it was not the family's main residence. It was, in fact, often regarded as the dower house of the estate in the next two centuries or so. Elizabeth Courtenay, widow both of Sir James Luttrell and of Sir Humphrey Audley (both of whom died in the Lancastrian cause) certainly had the manor as part of her dower, but only recovered it with difficulty (and with the help of the duke of Clarence) when Sir James's estates were confiscated. When finally the Herberts had been removed from the scene (see Dunster Castle) she had to contend with her son Hugh, who demanded land and the family silver to which he thought he was entitled. They finally agreed that she should retain East Quantoxhead and the silver for life, and the determined lady survived until 1493.

Top. Fireplace and overmantel in the Hall, dated 1629, with the arms and initials of George Luttrell.

Centre. Overmantel on the first floor showing Christ's Entry into Jerusalem.

Bottom. Overmantel in the Drawing Room showing Christ blessing the children.

Elizabeth's son Sir Hugh, perhaps because Dunster had been neglected by the Herbert intruders, seems to have preferred his mother's house and there is a family tradition (though no family accounts) to prove it. When he died in 1521 he was buried in the little church close beside the manor house, although the date on the much later tomb, carved when his heir Sir Andrew was buried beside him in 1538, is incorrect. And, like father like son, Sir Andrew was certainly living in the house when he drew up his will: 'of the parish of East Quantock', he described himself. Andrew's widow Margaret survived her husband for more than forty years, living in the house until her death in 1580.

When she died Margaret left some household goods and the former Priory estate at Dunster to her grandson George Luttrell, despite her opposition to his projected marriage. George, trained as a lawyer, proved a great builder, and it seems that it is to him that the Court House owes its present form, evidently as the result of two phases of building. The date 1614 is in one of the rooms above the old kitchens in the south range, and 1629 is on a fireplace in the hall in the east range, with the initials G.L.: 1629 was the year in which George Luttrell died.

Exactly what George built and what was there before is impossible to explain with certainty. The house lies too near the church for the south side ever to have been the front, but on that side is both a room known as the old kichen and, in the south-east corner, a three-storeyed tower which until the 19th century had a fourth storey. A defended house would have been entirely fitting for such a prominent and exposed position on its ridge overlooking the Bristol Channel shore. Running north from this tower is the thickest wall in the house, and there appears to be a medieval wing beyond the central courtyard to the west. George Luttrell may simply have rebuilt the east side of the original hall and added his prominent withdrawing room. Francis Luttrell is said to have added a room 'behind the kitchen' in 1689. The simplicity of George Luttrell's work, with its plain transomed windows, possibly an alteration of the later 17th century, is in striking contrast to the ornate carved stair and the overmantels, each showing a biblical scene so typical of the age – Christ and the Children, the Entry into Jerusalem, the Deposition, and the Ascension.

George Luttrell did not live to enjoy the fruits of his labours, but left his domineering widow Silvestra to make her new husband's life a misery and to outlive both her stepson, Thomas Luttrell, and Thomas's son and heir George. She died in 1655 and eventually a Luttrell in the person of Francis, George's brother, gained possession. Francis died in 1666 and was followed by his second son, also Francis (d. 1690), by Francis's young son Tregonwell (named after his mother's family), and in 1703 by Alexander Luttrell, Francis's younger brother.

The successive owners after the death of Dame Silvestra were also

The main, east front with the arched entrance under an earlier tower at the south-east corner.

owners of Dunster Castle and made that their principal residence. The house at East Quantoxhead seems to have been let as a farmhouse, and barns and a barton were built nearby. The traditions of the manor, as elsewhere on the Luttrell estates, were faithfully maintained. The court leet and baron still continued to meet in its 'ancient and customary place', for even though a Luttrell did not live in the manor house a Luttrell was certainly in the village, for the Revd. Alexander Fownes Luttrell was Rector between 1818 and 1888 and would surely have upheld such a worthy tradition in the unlikely event of tenants wishing otherwise. From 1865 until 1888, however, the 'customary place' was not available and the court met at the manor house, hence its 'modern' name, Court House.

That practice also came to an end in 1888 when Alexander Fownes Luttrell, heir to Dunster, took up residence there and remained until succeeding his father in 1910. His grandson, having made over the Dunster estates to the Crown in lieu of Death Duties, is the present Luttrell living in the ancestral home on the hill above the sea, surrounded by a garden which sets off the mellow stone of his manor house to perfection.

Dillington House

The visitor is quite likely to meet a tractor about its business, or a pheasant taking a leisurely stroll along one of the two drives leading to the house, for although Dillington is now no stately home for the exclusive pleasure of a landed proprietor it is still at the centre of a large and efficient agricultural operation. For forty years the mansion and its immediate surroundings have been leased to Somerset County Council, and for many thousands over those years it has been a magnet drawing old and young to educational courses and concerts, exhibitions and lectures and entertainments. Dillington has become, in those years, a way of life, a retreat where old friends gather and new ones are made. And the house, modest in its proportions but still with something far beyond the ordinary, welcomes those who pass through its doors as a kindly butler might put a visitor at ease with a gracious and dignified inclination of the head. Here is no wayward charm.

Today's student eats with the 'family' in the gracious dining room overlooking the lawn and the park. Two centuries and more ago, in 1768, a bankrupt Langport man borrowed a horse and rode over to see the then squire in the hope of mending his fortunes by acquiring a place. The suppliant was a man named Thomas Beedall whose only fame was to keep a diary which still survives. The squire was more than a squire, none other than Frederick North, Lord North, Tory M.P. for Banbury and Chancellor of the Exchequer. Beedall secured an interview, five guineas, and an enormous dinner with the head servants, as befitted his modest rank; and afterwards suffered a sleepless night.

Dillington was only Lord North's home by marriage, his wife Anne being the joint heiress with her sister of the Speke family and 'a lady of great fortune', some £4,000 a year. The Spekes had been in the district since the early 15th century. They arrived at Dillington in the person of George Speke who in 1599 bought the manor of West Dillington from Richard Bonville.

Just to make the story quite clear, in that same year another manor called West Dillington was in the possession of Robert Cuffe. Not only that, but half a century later probably both manors were let to tenant farmers whose land was in strips in East Dillington Field and Dillington Common Meadow and in small fields in West Dillington. Exactly where these fields lay is not clear, but there were also two other fields, Enforlong and Ilminster Field, which were in East

Frederick, Lord North, later Earl of Guilford (1732-1792), husband of Anne Speke of Dillington.

Dillington. It seems possible that the present hamlet of Dillington, scattered along the ridge above the park, is what remains of the two villages of East and West Dillington; and possible, too, that the house the Spekes bought from the Bonvilles still stands, now under the name of Dillington Farm. The Cuffe manor was sold in 1621 to John Manning, a yeoman farmer of Whitelackington, the village beyond the park to the east, and Mannings retained it until 1675. In 1719 another George Speke managed to buy it from the trustees of John Poole.

The Spekes were not just another small landowning clan, but in the 17th century played an important part in the history of Somerset. The George Speke, who in 1599 had bought West Dillington, died in 1637. His successor held the estate through the Civil War but in 1645 he was taken at Bridgwater and imprisoned in London. He secured his release on the grounds that he had been forced to join the king's army while still under age, but he was not entirely believed. He was fined £2,390 and was living under virtual house arrest in Wells in 1650. Under Charles II, however, he and his son John, both M.Ps in the 1679-81 parliament, found themselves among the 'County' opposition to the 'Court' party, in sympathy with those who wanted to exclude the Catholic Duke of York from the succession, and favoured instead the Protestant, if illegitimate, Duke of Monmouth. In 1680, when Monmouth came on his famous 'Progress' to the West, he was entertained in George Speke's park at Whitelackington, where the trunk of the tree under which he sat is still to be seen. Two years later the house at Whitelackington was searched in vain for arms, and when in 1685 Monmouth landed at Lyme Regis and marched with his army through Ilminster, John Speke led a troop of horse to join him and Charles, John's brother, greeted the duke with a handshake in Ilminster market place. When the rebellion failed George was left unmolested and John fled abroad, but Charles, on grounds which entirely satisfied Judge Jeffreys' notion of justice, was hanged because 'the family owe us a life'. George, the 'old rebel', survived until 1690 having by then thrown in his lot with William of Orange. The next George, son of John, was the purchaser of West Dillington in 1719.

Exactly what George the younger possessed is not clear, but it is certain that by 1768, the date of a schedule of the property which has survived, there had been created from farmland and two ancient scattered hamlets a classic piece of English parkland. There were still outlying farms on the estate including two farmhouses and seven cottages, one an inn called the Sun. At the heart of the estate was a mansion house set in ornamental grounds which included a 'figure walk', wilderness, sandy walk, nursery, herb garden, cherry orchard and islanded pond. Beyond the house was a park, then only recently formed since the names of the fields out of which it had been created were still remembered. To make that open grassland had involved the absorption of three small freeholds and the demolition of a house

The Conservatory.

The house with the remodelled south wing and conservatory.

— a modest enough price to pay, all things considered. Then or soon afterwards that green vista was enhanced by the creation of a canal, a rectangular stretch of water alongside the old road to Whitelackington. George Speke, presumably the creator, died in 1753.

The mansion at the time is not easy to describe, partly because suspicion must surround the earliest surviving features in the present house. It is known that John Lee Lee, owner from 1834, brought to Dillington from his home Barrington Court a number of fittings, oak floors and chimneys. Panelling in rooms in the north range is certainly not in its original position, nor yet is the door to the garden in the rear entrance passage. The panelling is Jacobean; the door, possibly contemporary with the plain screens and the window in the kitchen, suggests a mid 16th-century date. The range is certainly conventional in form, with kitchen to the east, central passage and room to the west. The unconventional lies in the floor levels, which may be the result of the later terracing when the front of the house was turned through ninety degrees.

Exactly when the modest farmhouse was thus transformed is a

matter for speculation. It must surely date from between 1719 and 1753. A description of the house at the end of the 18th century shows that it then had three storeys. The main rooms on the ground floor were a hall, vestibule, breakfast room, two 'eating' rooms and drawing room. 'Below stairs' were the housekeeper's room, butler's pantry, servants' hall, kitchen, scullery, larder and store. Two stair-cases led, the one to chambers on the first floor, the other direct to the servants' rooms in the attics. Immediately to the north across the road were the farmyard, stabling for thirty horses, ice house, laundry, brewhouse, cider house and hen house; and gardens, green-houses, fishponds and the gardener's house. This was the establish-ment where Mr Beedall had his interview in Lord North's room (by repute – but perhaps only a fancy of a former Head of the College – on the first floor at the north-west corner). This was the establish-ment where at 5 o'clock he dined with the head servants 'and had for dinner a Dish of fish, a sirloyn of Beef roasted, a Loyn of Veal with collyflowers, carrotts etc. for the first course, and for the second a roast Turkey, a hare, pigeon pye, fried oysters, chicken Tarts, Lavor etc. Drank water at dinner, after Dinner drank 4 glasses of Port wine'.

What the family ate Mr Beedall did not know, but he did note that after dinner 'there came into the room his Lordship's youngest son, Master Frederick, about 2 years and half old, a fine boy'. That fine boy on the deaths of his father and his older brothers, succeeded to the earldom of Guilford in 1817. Several years before that, however, in 1795 the family trustees sold Dillington, Whitelackington and other Somerset lands for the sum of £83,000 to John Hanning of Barrington Court, son of a remarkably prosperous tenant farmer, who managed to find an initial payment of £52,000. It is probable that either John, who died in 1803, or his son William, who died in 1825, made further alterations to the house, including a plain, one-storeyed south wing with sash windows to the west and a curious curved pediment facing south. This is clearly shown in the accurate elevation made in 1837 and the less accurate engraving of 1831. By that time, indeed by the time a plan of the estate was made for William Han-ning in 1824, the approach to the house was intentionally dramatic, beginning at the lodges on Bay Hill in Ilminster, sweeping between trees over the hill and curving round to the formal west front.

To William Hanning's son John belong the changes which created the symmetrical neo-Tudor house which now stands. William had achieved some social status by acquiring a patent of arms; his son, succeeding an uncle, Major John Lee of Orleigh Court, Devon, took his name and was thereafter known as John Lee Lee. In the year he succeeded his father at Dillington, 1834, he also raised £50,000 by way of mortgage. Some of that may well have been spent on transforming a rather irregular and incongruous house into a building which, at least from its external faces, is a delight, Gothic in spirit, Barrington with a touch of Regency. The ugly south wing was replaced by one to balance the north, the hall windows were

Two drawings of 1837, possibly by
James Pennethorne, showing the single
storey addition to the west wing and the
curious south-facing curved pediment
added by John or William Hanning
between 1795 and 1825.

regularised. The forecourt and the terrace were formalised with
balustrading, all, presumably (for only two drawings are now known)
the work of the young James Pennethorne (1801-71), pupil of both
Nash and Pugin. Not all his suggestions were carried out, for plans
signed by him included an extension to the north wing, flanked by
twin towers, to provide stables and a billiard room.

John Lee Lee lived at Dillington until his death in 1874. His son
Vaughan Hanning Lee took the additional surname Vaughan when
he succeeded to the Welsh estates of his mother Jessie Edwards
Vaughan of Lanelay and Rheola. He lived at Dillington from 1874
until 1882 and contributed the great stable block, now the college
theatre complex, and containing besides stables, a coach house, ken-
nels, laundry and staff quarters. The design was by George Nat-
tress of London and cost on completion in 1875 £5,512 12s 3d. Mr
Vaughan-Lee is remembered as a disciplinarian, incarcerating small
boys in the cellars or ice house when caught trespassing, and in-
sisting on having them chastised by their parents before he would
release them.

The ceiling of the Dining Room.

Inventories of the contents of the house made in 1874 and 1882 reveal a typical house of the period. The public rooms were modest and are easy to recognise today: drawing room, library, hall, dining room, morning room and conservatory. On the first floor there were fourteen bedrooms with dressing rooms, work room, bathroom and two water closets. Above were four more bedrooms and four attic rooms. The staff house to the north was added by 1882. Behind the new stable block in 1882 were a workshop, sawpit, wash house, potting house, fruit house and four hot houses in the walled garden. The contents of the cellar in 1882 included 175 dozen claret, 87 dozen champagne, 72 dozen sherry, 64 dozen port and 49 dozen hock.

In 1882 Vaughan Hanning Vaughan-Lee was succeeded at Dillington and Lanelay by his son Arthur, later Colonel of the Royal Horse Guards, who served with his regiment in the South African war. He was well known as a sportsman, notably at polo. He died in 1933 and was followed by his daughter, Mrs Elizabeth Cameron. In 1950 she leased the house and its immediate grounds to Somerset County Council as a residential college.

Students who come to the college find they want to return again and again, not just because of the quality of the teaching but also for the character of the house. The mellow walls and intimate garden will continue to draw a wide public who come to appreciate Dillington's undoubted grace.

Dunster Castle

A building which can claim at once to have been the principal Somerset castle at the time of Domesday and one of the most popular National Trust properties in the later 20th century deserves to be praised. Yet in the long period since Domesday the building has radically changed in character. It is still called Dunster Castle, but it has effectively been a country house rather than a military stronghold since the early 17th century.

The castle was built on a natural site, chosen by William Mohun in the 11th century. Mohun's stronghold was the adaptation of the top of that site as a motte. Still surviving from the later buildings are the lower part of the 13th-century north gateway and Sir Hugh Luttrell's Barbican; and parts of the walls of the main house were castle walls earlier. Archaeology would undoubtedly reveal more of the fortress which defied King Stephen in 1138 and which was modified by Mohuns and Luttrells during the Middle Ages. By the early 16th century the buildings in the upper ward were in poor repair except a chapel. In the fortified lower ward, 'the fairest part of the castelle welle maintenid', as Leland wrote in the 1540s, were the principal apartments arranged in a single block not unlike a keep. The rest of the castle had suffered not in siege nor frontal attack but from the neglect of temporary owners, the Herberts, hirelings rather than the true shepherds, whose tenure came about by the attainder of Sir James Luttrell during the Wars of the Roses.

Sir James had fallen fighting for his king at the second battle of St Albans in 1460; the failure of Henry VI had made his loyal supporter a rebel. Luttrell lands were seized and given to the Yorkist Sir William Herbert, Baron Herbert and later Earl of Pembroke. The Herberts enjoyed possession of the castle until Henry Tudor came to power after Bosworth in 1485. There is no direct evidence that the castle had been neglected by the Herberts, but Sir Hugh Luttrell, Sir James's son, clearly preferred to live at East Quantoxhead; and his son, Thomas, permitted others to occupy rooms in the 'Inner Pyle or Lodginges'.

Thomas's successor George Luttrell converted what remained of the medieval castle into a country mansion. The thick curtain wall was retained and so were two towers, but within that general frame, with considerable ingenuity considering the sloping site, he built a mansion fit for the squire of Dunster and owner of wide acres in West Somerset. Mullioned and transomed windows were inserted in the

The Barbican, built by Sir Hugh Luttrell (died 1428).

former defences and a facade in red stone and dressed quoins created elegant domesticity where once there had been military pragmatism. Thus was formed a house of three storeys, the ground floor comprising a hall roughly where the inner hall now stands, a parlour and a little parlour, all at the north-eastern end of the building, with a later library block and offices at the other end and chambers above. From that house there still survive the plasterwork of the hall ceiling and the gallery frieze. The date 1589 under a large coat of arms in the hall perhaps marks the completion of one stage of a long task.

Its end came more than thirty years later when in a lawsuit in Chancery George Luttrell had to explain why he had not paid William Arnold what he owed. His answer was that Arnold, architect of Wadham College, Oxford, and of Cranborne Manor, and possibly also designer of Montacute, having produced a 'plot' and an 'upright', had not only changed the plan after approval but had changed it again as work progressed; and further still, that his estimated cost of £462 was likely to rise to £1,200. The date 1620 on an overmantel with strapwork and caryatids is certainly an indication that work continued after the lawsuit had somehow been concluded.

Arnold produced out of an unpromising and constricted site a house of remarkable symmetry which had a facade with a porch-tower in the middle of a central range flanked by two two-bay wings, and with a tower in each angle thus formed. Only the floors were somewhat irregular. Comfort had arrived and with it, perhaps, convenience. The present National Trust shop below the gatehouse began life in the earlier 17th century as stabling for 28 horses.

Thomas Luttrell, son of George, like many Somerset gentry, was for Parliament. He garrisoned his home in 1642 and held it until June 1643 when Royalists under Sir Francis Wyndham persuaded him to yield in the face of Parliament's loss of Taunton and Bridgwater. Either as an earnest of his loyalty to the Crown or as recompense for his previous actions he was obliged to pay £1,000 to the king. Thomas's rather formidable wife paid a further £1,500 on behalf of herself and her sons after her husband's death in 1644.

The castle and its Royalist garrison sheltered Prince Charles for a fortnight in May 1645 but by the summer it was the only place in the county held for the king. The challenge was taken up and Robert Blake laid siege to it in November. Mining destroyed a part of the wall but Wyndham held out gallantly until the middle of April 1646. Thereafter for five years the castle was garrisoned and Thomas's heir, another George Luttrell, had to share his home with a military governor. In 1650 orders were given that the castle 'be so farre slighted as that it may not be made suddainely teneable by an enemy'. Two hundred men spent 12 days demolishing the walls and the buildings around the keep and defacing the gatehouse. The mansion house was saved because it was in use as a gaol for William Prynne, the notorious political pamphleteer, who had managed to incur the displeasure first of Archbishop Laud and later of the Commonwealth.

Thomas Luttrell (1584-1644), last owner of the medieval castle at Dunster.

The oak and elm staircase, part of the improvements made by Colonel Francis Luttrell (died 1690).

The south-east range, with the ornate chapel designed by Sir James Thornhill, drawn in 1839.

Prynne spent his time organizing George Luttrell's archives on a basis which still obtains. George's support for the new government was later so far acknowledged that the garrison was removed.

The property became a home again and successive owners left their mark on its structure and decoration. To Colonel Francis Luttrell (died 1690) is owed the elaborate plaster ceiling of the Parlour, its frieze bearing the arms of his wife Mary Tregonwell and the date 1681. He also contributed the magnificent Great Staircase in oak and elm, its richly carved foliage, hunting cherubs and military trophies a fine tribute to the man who played a significant part in the peaceful accession of William of Orange and in the formation of a local regiment of which he was the first colonel – the regiment which later became the 19th Foot and is now the Green Howards. In the colonel's time the staircase continued as a gallery over part of the hall.

Improvements in the 18th century included a new approach from Dunster village around the east side of the hill avoiding the steep approach under the ancient gateways. These were the work of Dorothy Luttrell in 1720. She also built, under the direction of Sir James Thornhill, an elaborate chapel on the site of one of the eastern towers; it was unfinished at her death in 1723. At about the same time any buildings left on the site of the original keep were removed

to make way for a bowling green, whose summer house bears the date 1727.

Surviving inventories show that the famous Spanish or Portuguese leather hangings of Anthony and Cleopatra came to Dunster between 1705 and 1737, and in 1744 they were valued at £21. They added an exotic flavour to a house already a curious mixture of Medieval Military and Late-Tudor Domestic, tinged with Thornhill Flamboyant. And then a new owner, Henry Fownes, who could trace his ancestry back to the Mohuns who first built the castle (a claim the Luttrells could not make) took the hand and name of Margaret Luttrell and promised her father he would live at Dunster for six months every year.

Henry Fownes Luttrell finally converted the castle into a country

Above. The Leather Room, with the Portuguese leather hangings of Anthony and Cleopatra which were acquired by the Luttrells in the early 18th century.

Opposite. The north-west front. The drawing of 1839 by J. Buckler shows the front designed by William Arnold for Thomas Luttrell (died 1644). The photograph shows Anthony Salvin's mid 19th-century alterations for Henry Fownes Luttrell, including the kitchen tower to the left of the entrance porch.

house, not so much by his alterations to the house as to changes he made in the grounds, placing the building in a context of elegance by planting trees to the south and east, creating the deer park, and building the tower on Conigar Hill in 1775. Inside the house his changes were relatively minor, concerned mostly with decorating the rooms in contemporary style, blocking up or adding a few windows, and remodelling the servants' quarters on the south side.

One other, and major, external change radically altered the grounds immediately in front of the house; the level lawns are Henry Fownes Luttrell's creation, designed by Thomas Hull to make access to the house more convenient for carriages. The original lower ward, which had sloped away from the front of the house, was thus created by means of hundreds of tons of earth, into the Green Court, completed in 1764. At the same time Sir Hugh Luttrell's fine gatehouse, partly buried on one side by the new works, was given polygonal turrets and made to look like a gatehouse entrance which gives access in fact to the second floor of the original structure. The genuine door and doorway were found elsewhere on the site. The whole work was, from a domestic point of view, an undoubted improvement. Archaeologically, more of the medieval remains of the castle were either buried or destroyed.

Henry Fownes Luttrell's work in the house was to last for three generations almost unaltered, until George Fownes Luttrell succeeded his uncle in 1867. He came into possession of an estate of well over 15,000 acres in Somerset and nearly 2,000 in Devon, and of a house which clearly needed attention. Anthony Salvin produced for Mr Luttrell a series of rooms which his contemporaries would no doubt have envied had they been arranged within Victorian walls. Salvin's genius was to use the space available to its best advantage for the requirements of a Victorian squire – billiard room, justice room, library, conservatory – largely within the confines of ancient walls. Externally Salvin was more radical, creating with new towers and an irregular skyline elevations which make Dunster the epitome of Victorian medievalism. Arnold's regular entrance front became distinctly irregular with the addition of the massive kitchen tower. An outer hall was formed, immediately imposing on the visitor an impression of the grandeur within. Thornhill's fussy chapel became another massive tower to house a drawing room.

Salvin's towers, rising above the trees on its tor are now a good deal less threatening than the stronghold of William Mohun, a good deal less impregnable even than the house defended for so long in the Civil War. The rare shrubs in the garden thrive on terraces which were once too steep to permit an assault, although the popularity of the house today might bring a wry smile from the Royalist commander who kept the besiegers at bay for 160 days. For today the castle is in the care of the National Trust, since the Luttrells were forced to leave through the more insidious pressures of the cost of inheritance.

George Fownes Luttrell (1826-1910), Salvin's patron at Dunster in the 1860s.

Enmore Castle

John Perceval, second Earl of Egmont in the Peerage of Ireland, politician, pamphleteer and powerful debater, had a vision of the past. His father, the first earl, employed two genealogists to establish that the Percevals were descendants of William, Baron of Yvery, at the beginning of the 12th century. Boswell was impressed at the way in which 'the noble Lord' had 'honoured and perpetuated his ancestry', but Lord Dover called the work 'a remarkable monument of human vanity'. A more modern genealogist has described much of it as 'an impudent fiction'. It is said to have cost the family £3,000 in fees alone to the College of Arms.

Fiction or not, the influence of the Tory Lord Bute obtained for the second earl political power and an English barony with the resoundingly medieval title of Baron Lovel and Holland of Enmore in the county of Somerset.

If Lord Egmont's claim was spurious in purist eyes, his connection with Somerset was not, for Percevals could be traced back to Tickenham in the Middle Ages, and they had built and occupied the impressive little manor house at Sydenham on the eastern side of Bridgwater. Back in the 16th century Richard Perceval's skill with languages had ensured his fortune, for he had deciphered and translated the secret letters relating to the Armada, and had been lavishly rewarded with offices and land in Ireland. But the Percevals had left Sydenham early in the 17th century, and their return to their native county was probably for political reasons, namely the search for a secure seat in the English Parliament to ensure a political future.

The exact course of events is not clear, but in 1736 the corporation of Bridgwater chose the young John Perceval, then styled Viscount Perceval, to be a burgess, the first clear evidence of the family's political influence in the town and the first step on the way to election to Parliament. But the real motive was carefully concealed: the burgesses chose him to be one of their number, they declared in their official minutes, 'for his great merits and knowledge in antiquities and useful learning'. That he had such merits and knowledge is not in question; he was elected a Fellow of the Society of Antiquaries of London in the same year.

The next steps are less certain, but it is clear that, after the death of his father in 1748, Egmont associated himself strongly with the Prince of Wales, and secured an appointment as a Lord of the Bedchamber. The prospect of real power beckoned. Still, his seat in the

House of Commons was not secure since he had offended its patron; by purchasing what remained of the manor of Enmore from the Baynton family he could continue what his father had begun, the creation of a power base at Bridgwater.

Egmont's purchase of land at Enmore put him into a long historical succession. For generation after generation at least since the mid 12th century, Enmore had been the home of the Malets, a family of prominence in Somerset's history. The last Malet of Enmore was Elizabeth, daughter of John Malet, whom at least three peers of the realm sought in marriage. A fourth, the wit and rake John Wilmot, Earl of Rochester, married her after spending some time in the Tower of London for trying to carry her off by force.

Much of the Malet estate had been sold off by the Bayntons after an Act of Parliament in 1742 was passed to pay off their debts, and Egmont bought what was left. If anything remained of the hall or chapel of the medieval Malets, we do not know, but there was still what was called a 'Great House' on the estate, later called the Gatehouse, standing on an ancient site which, when adapted would be entirely suitable for the residence of a prospective Prime Minister. But then his plans went seriously awry, for the Prince of Wales died; the prospect of political power disappeared, and Egmont's only consolation was his second obsession, his passion for the feudal and medieval. Enmore was to be the site of a castle to which none of the Malets had ever aspired, and between 1751 and 1755 the building, probably incorporating that gatehouse, was created.

It was a remarkable creation, a vast four-square, incredibly feudal affair in reddish, dark-coloured stone, designed by Egmont himself. In form it was a huge square keep rising to four square towers at each corner, capped with machicolations and battlements. At the centre of three sides were massive, semi-circular turrets, similarly capped, and on the fourth was a pair of towers forming a gatehouse. This mass of masonry provided suites of rooms arranged around a hollow measuring 86 feet by 78 feet.

The rooms were on four floors, but until the visitor approached quite close, only three were visible. Beneath was a basement set in a vast walled enclosure giving the impression of a wide moat, dry save for an L-shaped stew pond constructed in each corner. This basement included servants' quarters, cellarage, an evidence room, a laundry and a confectioner's room. Some of the servants' rooms were later converted to stables. Heavy goods and horses were brought to this basement level by means of a graduated tunnel, its entrance carefully concealed in a fold of the surrounding park.

The next floor, level with the park and entered across the 'moat' via a drawbridge complete with lifting devices, contained the entrance gateway into the central courtyard. From there the grand entrance gave access to the Armoury and Dining Room and the grand staircase to the floor above. On one side of the court were several suites of bedrooms, on the other the kitchen and larders, halls

Opposite. The castle in 1783, showing the entrance into the principal floors over the drawbridge and the adjoining parish church.

Below. A drawing of the drawbridge machinery at Enmore Castle.

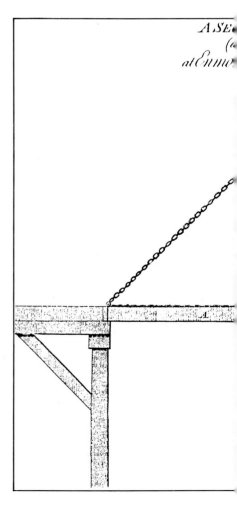

DRAW BRIDGE and *MACHINERY*
(same is very Easily raised & let down)
Seat of the R.ᵗ Hon.ᵇˡᵉ The Earl of Egmont

By a Scale of one Quarter of an Inch to a Foot.

for the servants, the housekeeper's room, the butler's pantry and the steward's counting house. Above was the principal floor, including the Great Hall, State Room, Long Gallery, Library, Dining Room and Saloon, more bedchambers and the Cabinet. The top floor comprised only nurseries and upper servants' rooms above the Great Hall. In total there were nearly seventy rooms.

Around his castle Lord Egmont planned a great park. Like many of his contemporaries, he wanted to create vistas where the only Art required to enhance Nature was the art of removing tenants as far away as possible. The village street of Enmore was obviously too near his Lordship's door and, besides, it was also a busy route from Bridgwater to the Quantocks. So, despite opposition from various quarters, his Lordship induced the turnpike trustees in 1759 to obtain an Act of Parliament for a new line of road, actually only a short distance from the original course but conveniently below the crest of the ridge and thus beyond his Lordship's gaze. Enmore church and village were thus for a time standing in vulnerable isolation. The next steps cannot now be traced very clearly, but in 1767 Egmont bought that part of the churchyard on the Castle side of the church and added that to the park, as well as diverting roads and paths as he pushed out the park boundary in other directions.

Lord Egmont died in 1770 and his successor, also John, continued his work on the park, buying up and demolishing houses in the village street in the 1780s and the early 1790s and offering alternative housing elsewhere on the estate. He even took over and demolished the parsonage house, exchanged land outside the park for the parson's glebe inside it, and built a new house for the rector inconveniently far away. In the first few years of the 19th century more houses were demolished by the hated agent, nicknamed 'Squire Cruckshanks'. Opponents claimed that smaller tenants were being removed and that the parish would soon have no-one but labourers and beggars. But within twenty years all this dream came to an end. In 1833 the fourth earl and his heir faced ruin as the result of lawsuits in which, over a number of years, they had had to find over £180,000 not counting costs. The whole estate was therefore put up for sale in 105 lots, the first being the Castle and Park.

In the event about 5,000 acres were sold as a single unit for £135,000 to Henry Labouchère, then M.P. for Taunton and a rising politician. The Castle and Park were disposed of for £28,000 to Nicholas Broadmead of Milverton. The sale of the contents took place early in 1834. The list of furniture and fittings, arranged room by room as they were found, reveals little about the style of decoration; they were simply Chintz, Green, Yellow or Blue rooms, although a room and two passages on the west side of the house were stuccoed and two bedrooms were fitted into alcoves on the south side. One recent creation seems to have been a billiard room, and there were galleries for both pictures and music. Lord Egmont's dressing room, Lady Catherine's bedroom (possibly named after Catherine, first wife of the second earl and daughter of the Earl of Salisbury), and Lord Rochester's cabinet were the only rooms where the members of the family seem to have left their names. But the house contained mementoes of another kind. The second earl's connection with the Prince of Wales explained the painted chair, a workbox and some china formerly belonging to Queen Caroline, the Prince's mother. The third earl's Tory principles perhaps accounted for the coffee pot which once belonged to Princess Caroline, the rejected wife of the Prince Regent.

Otherwise, there seem to have been few choice possessions offered for sale; the auctioneer thought to mention especially busts of Sir John and Lady Perceval by Vincentius Felix of 1707, an apparently 'ancient' tapestry of Queen Elizabeth, and some other tapestries of Classical scenes. These last found their way first to Combe Sydenham House, Monksilver, and in 1950 three were bought for the Council Chamber at Bridgwater. They thus returned to the borough which had elected the building earl to their corporation two centuries earlier. Two helms displayed in the church at Enmore probably came from the castle Armoury.

After the contents had been disposed of Mr Broadmead set about making Lord Egmont's pile into a house. His plan was radical, nothing less than the demolition of the buildings on the north, east and south sides of the central court and the creation of a vaguely Classical building from the remaining wing. Egmont's curious and small 'baronial' windows were everywhere replaced by sashes, square on the second floor, round-headed on the others, the whole under a low-pitched and slated roof with deep eaves. Only the staircase retained anything of the form of Egmont's semi-circular towers. The

Right. The south front from the original central courtyard.

Below. The west front of the surviving house from the 'moat' showing the deep eaves which replaced the crenellations in the 1830s.

flavour of the whole was emphasised in detail: one of the pair of Drawing Rooms was Ionic, the other Corinthian according to a contemporary plan; and the main east front had a two-storeyed colonnade in Doric style. Two roundels on that east front, carved with the Perceval arms, were obvious reminders of the former owners, but much of the mid-18th-century detail was preserved inside Mr Broadmead's new home. This was obviously more modest in scale, with drawing and breakfast rooms, a justice room and a water closet on the 'ground' floor over the still almost complete underground stables and offices. Above were six bedrooms with dressing rooms, a large library with a coved and ornamented ceiling, and another water closet.

This house remained within a much reduced park a Broadmead possession for a century, but before 1936 Harold Hamilton Broadmead reduced its size and remodelled it inside and out. In the 1950s the house was divided into two dwellings.

It was the considered opinion of at least one neighbouring landowner that Egmont's house was 'a very ugly ill built concern'. It was undoubtedly the product of a romantic imagination and a long purse. Lord Egmont would himself have approved of the Archery Fete which took place there in July 1844, although by that time the Castle bore almost no relation to the medieval pile which would have provided the ladies and gentlemen with such an appropriate back drop for their activities. Lord Rosebery once described Lord Egmont as 'an able man not without incredible absurdities'. Enmore Castle might well have been one of these.

Fairfield

Thomas Palmer, a gentleman of antiquarian bent and evidently scrupulous fairness, drew up his will in July 1733. He was then only fifty but already smitten with the 'calamitous illness' which was soon to kill him. He was almost the last of his line, for he and his wife had no children; neither had his younger brother Peregrine, nor his five sisters. The likely heir to his family estates was a young man named Arthur Acland, not only his wife's nephew but also husband (such were commonly the links between landed families) of one of his own rather distant cousins. But Thomas recognised in his will that he owed his prosperity rather to his wife than to his own inheritance, for she was heiress to the estates of the Wroths. So in leaving a modest sum of money to his brother and sisters he acknowledged that it was his own dear Elizabeth's fortune he was spending, and that for the rest, in case he survived her, he felt himself 'in conscience obliged to make her the best return I can, which is to give her the entire possession of an estate redeemed by her own generosity . . . and therefore let no one blame me if, in so doing, I have put an end to my own family'.

The heirs, of course, made sure that his name did not die, and the father of the present owner bore the name Palmer as had many of his forebears. Thomas Palmer's contribution was not just to the future of his heritage, for among the family archives are papers in his own careful if rather small handwriting, the product of many hours of study in the Evidence Room at Fairfield. There he had pored over charters which generations of owners had left behind in his search not only for the history of his own family and estate, but for a more ambitious undertaking, to write the first history of Somerset.

Among the oldest charters at Fairfield was one dating from the late 12th century by which Maud de Chandos, lady of Nether Stowey, divided some land which a tenant named Goslan had once held from her. Goslan had certainly been alive in 1166, but now his holding was to be shared between his son Martin of Fairfield and Walter de Castello. Between 1212 and 1216 William Russel was given Martin's tenancy, and from that time Fairfield has been owned by William's descendants.

There have, over that long time, been several changes of name among the owners as Russel was succeeded by Verney, Verney by Palmer, and Palmer, soon after Thomas's death, by Acland. In 1818 the then owner of Fairfield — and of much else besides — John Acland, on receiving a baronetcy, assumed the additional name of Palmer, presumably in recognition of his ancestry. John's son Peregrine in 1834 also took the name of Fuller from his mother's family. Sir Peregrine Fuller-Palmer-Acland, to give him his full name, had an only daughter Isabel. Her precarious health threatened the family line, but the bracing air of the sea which she enjoyed while living for several months in a wooden house built for her on the cliffs at nearby Lilstock, secured her recovery.

The Fairfield estates went with her hand to Alexander Hood who, shortly before their marriage in 1849, assumed the Fuller-Acland names from his bride-to-be. Sir Alexander Fuller-Acland-Hood (1853-1917), their son and the fourth baronet in succession through his father from the naval Hoods, was a landowner and Conservative politician, serving in the administrations of Lord Salisbury and A.J. Balfour successively as Vice-Chamberlain of the Household and Patronage Secretary to the Treasury (Chief Whip) between 1900 and 1905. He sat as M.P. for West Somerset for sixteen years, retiring in 1911 when he was created Baron St Audries after the home not far from Fairfield where he lived. Peregrine, the second baron, died unmarried in 1967 leaving Fairfield to his niece Elizabeth, then Elizabeth Acland-Hood and now Lady Gass.

Fairfield has been for the author a place of discoveries: the first time it was a long-lost tiara which had somehow been buried under a mound of almost abandoned estate records; then the iron door and grille, more suited to a prison than to a country house, behind which local offenders might be confined to await the constable after judgement by an Acland Justice of the Peace. Finally, armed by the owner with an offensive weapon to hack away parts of the plaster ceiling in the 19th-century attics of the south-west wing, were revealed what Sir John Acland had wished to hide – nothing less than the decorated roof timbers of a late-medieval first-floor hall.

The Reverend Richard Warner, walking through the Western Counties in about 1800, thought Fairfield 'a large but tasteless building, the product of the 16th century when architecture was sunk to its lowest ebb'. He credited Thomas Palmer with beginning the house on an ancient site about 1580, although if the date is correct, then it must have been Thomas's mother, Elizabeth (née Verney) who was responsible. The work was still unfinished in 1633. But what Elizabeth did was to remodel a house already a century old, a house still existing under that richly decorated roof and around the blocked doorway which has puzzled so many visitors in the former screens passage.

In those searches in his Evidence Room Thomas Palmer in the 18th century noted something which for all his care has not survived. It was a licence, granted to William Verney by the king about 1473 to build a wall and seven round towers to defend his house. Three of those towers still stood on the boundary of a walled court to the east of the house in Thomas Palmer's time, but no trace of them can now

Opposite top. Fairfield, the park and house, an engraving published in 1791.

Opposite bottom. The south front facing the park.

Below. Some of the finely-carved late-medieval timbers of the first-floor Hall in the west range.

The Saloon, with ancestral portraits and part of the coved ceiling.

be found. They would, of course, have made Fairfield more like the traditional castle than the gracious country house which it has become.

However, the recent discovery of a map of Stogursey drawn for a neighbouring landowner has suggested a new interpretation for the development of the house. It was drawn in 1610 by a careful cartographer and shows quite clearly a building with irregular ranges around four sides of a courtyard with tall, substantial chimneys. Perhaps what made Thomas Gerard think the house was unfinished in 1633 was that part of the building was then being demolished. It is now an 'E' shaped house, and perhaps regarded in the 18th century as a little plain, but with a central entrance porch under a three-storeyed tower topped by a decorative roof. It was very far from tasteless.

There is one other curiosity about the house: it lies partly in Stogursey parish and partly in Lilstock. The original house was in Lilstock, and when John Verney was heavily fined in 1498 for his support of the puppet-rebel Perkin Warbeck, his £40 was collected in Lilstock's Honibere tithing. An earlier rebellious Verney, another John, had been so bold as to stand up in the priory church in Stogursey exhorting the congregation to take no notice of the prior and the parish priest. An even earlier member of the family, Henry Verney, had held Stogursey castle on behalf of the unpleasant and overwheening Fawkes de Breauté, then lord of the manor, in 1224.

A detail from a map of 1610 of the Earl of Northumberland's estate at Stogursey, showing Fairfield as a medieval courtyard house.

The 17th century thatched barn.

Clearly much of the present house is the work of the Palmers and the Aclands. The antiquarian Thomas Palmer or his father Nathaniel (died 1718) put in the present staircase. About 1780 and again about 1815 Sir John Acland spent a good deal of money, demolishing some rooms on the south-west and building a new kitchen behind the hall, to be served, like the rest of the house, by servants who were able to move through narrow staircases and passages and never be seen by the family and their guests. Many of the rooms were then newly decorated, the hall given its coved ceiling and probably the chandelier which the present owner's father discovered how to swing, much to the surprise of assembled guests. The walls of that hall are lined with portraits of Palmers and Hoods, a fine display of family history.

The same Sir John Acland also created the park in front of Fairfield. In the early 18th century there had been that essential landscape feature, a short canal, providing a stretch of water before the house, but unfortunately divided from it by the high road from Stogursey to Stringston. Sir John made a new road away from the house, building lodges at two entrances and planting the trees which still grace the park today. The grounds include a fine walled garden whose wall is dated 1784, a 17th-century barn, and an 18th-century granary. A woodland garden with bulbs and shrubs is the worthy contribution of the 20th century.

Gothelney, Gurney Street Manor and Blackmoor Farm

Gothelney. The tall house, with its upper Great Chamber, ornate porch and imposing tower, was probably built by William Hody in the late 15th century. The engraving shows the house in 1845, prior to the building of the wing on the right.

Three houses standing within a mile or two of each other near Cannington between the Quantocks and the Parrett illustrate as clearly as any written record the prosperity that comes from competent practice of the law. Three houses, probably built within a few years of each other in the last thirty years of the 15th century, a century when lawyers had demonstrated how the legal process was both a support and a hindrance in a cause, however righteous; a century when one who could take advantage of what passed for English justice was well worth his retainers and his fees.

The most remarkable of these three houses is Gothelney, in the parish of Charlinch, and its builders were remarkable, too. Adam Hody, great grandfather of the probable builder, was a peasant, bound to his lord by virtue of his birth. Of his two sons, John amassed a small fortune as a clerical lawyer, Thomas administered the Luttrell estates. The cleric, having no sons, sent his brother's children to school and then bought their legal freedom. Both became lawyers in their turn, Sir John Hody rising to be Chief Justice of the King's Bench for a little over a year until his death in 1441. His brother Alexander, steward for several West Country landowners including the Earl of Salisbury and retained counsel of the burgesses of Bridgwater, represented Shaftesbury, Bridgwater or Somerset in Parliament at least ten times. A Lancastrian in politics, he fought under the Earl of Devon at the battle of Wakefield in 1460 but died after Towton in the following year. As an enemy of the new Yorkist regime he was attainted, but Gothelney seems to have been safe, since by 1455 he had moved to West Bower, nearer Bridgwater, where some window glass still bears his initials.

William Hody, Alexander's nephew, succeeded to Gothelney. A lawyer of the third generation, he was appointed sergeant at law and attorney general in 1485 and was Chief Baron of the Exchequer from 1486 to 1522. He was active locally as a Justice of the Peace from 1470 and he is the likeliest builder of the fine house. It is a puzzling and unusual building whose precise dating is impossible. Its obvious feature is its height and its three-storeyed tower beside an ornate porch. The tower, somewhat later than the main range, has a remarkable anti-clockwise spiral stair and a possible oratory or chapel on its top storey. In the main range was a single room in the normal hall position, above which was an upper hall or great chamber, originally lit by tall transomed windows with cinquefoiled heads and with a magnificent arch-braced roof. Its main trusses are supported on angel corbels. At the south end of these great rooms, behind the tower, is a four-storeyed section with a similar, two-bay roof.

The main house has a lower range to the south and was probably built in the 16th century, perhaps still in Sir William Hody's time. The east range, running from the south end of the hall, seems to contain elements of the original kitchen and may well have housed retainers and servants. The north wing belongs to the 17th century.

Throughout this long period of complicated development the Hodys still lived at Gothelney, but rather as gentlemen farmers hardly to be distinguished from their neighbours. The lawyer syndrome had evidently been spent. John Hody sold his ancestral home to Roger Bourne in 1622; and Babers followed by Gores stayed here until 1864. The house was requisitioned during the Second World War and was later used as a kindergarten. It is now cherished as a family home, a dwelling tied to the estate on which it stands.

Just a mile to the north is a house whose glories are only now, after great cost to the Landmark Trust, being revealed. For many years divided into flats and with a scantily-recorded history, Gurney Street Manor is now amply repaying attention.

Named, obviously enough, after the Gurney family who held land in this part of Cannington in the 14th century, the estate came into the hands of a family of obvious energy and competence who had begun building a land-holding nearby in the later 14th century. William Dodesham died in 1440 meriting a brass inscription in his parish church. His son, also William, an attorney and once Member of Parliament for Bridgwater, made his memorial the beginnings of Gurney Street Manor.

The building is arranged around four sides of a courtyard, its

Gurney Street Manor. A watercolour by W.W. Wheatley dated 1845 showing the west side of the house, including the parlour, solar and chapel.

Gurney Street Manor. The restored solar wing and kitchen.

front having protruding wings which form a north-facing shallow forecourt. The north range contained the hall, of which very little still remains beyond its outline. To the west was a parlour which was rebuilt and extended as a solar block and included a small chapel. This new work must have been undertaken by Thomas Michell, owner between 1503 and 1539. Thomas 'was a man of great possessions & estemyd to have at the tyme of his death goods and catalls to the value of on[e] thousand poundes & aboue'. Those possessions, the furnishings of his house and contents of his farm, all had to be sold, for on 13 December 1539 there was a great family tragedy: Thomas first killed his sister-in-law Eleanor Sydenham, then his wife Joan, and finally himself.

The rest of the family somehow survived. Richard Michell (died 1563) was followed by his son Tristram (died 1574), and Tristram by his brother Sir Bartholomew (died 1616). To Tristram or Bartholomew probably belong the new windows on the west side, plaster work in the chapel, and a lobby with a bridge which gave access to the first floor of the kitchen range to the south. Bartholomew perhaps added an upper floor in the hall and divisions below, and probably the west range. He may also have built the curious covered way across the courtyard to give his servants some protection as they made their way from kitchen to hall or parlour.

Later owners with estates elsewhere seem to have left the house to tenant farmers, protecting it from changes by landlords' well-known reluctance to spend money on improvements. Hockmores of Buckland Baron in Devon gave place to Goulds, the last of whom married Richard Lambart, Earl of Cavan. Successive earls owned it for a century until 1925. Now the layers of paper, paint and plaster have been peeled painstakingly away, timbers restored or replaced. Soon the Landmark Trust will be welcoming temporary tenants wishing to enjoy on holiday a little vicarious pleasure from the profits of the law.

On the other side of Cannington, down a quiet lane, is Blackmoor Farm, a house much more simply understood and externally hardly changed over three centuries. Lawyers then had their fingers in many peoples' affairs, and John Kenne, the owner, first leased his manor to William Hody of Gothelney in 1475 and then sold it in 1476 through the agency of William Dodesham to Thomas Tremayll, thus completing a curious legal triumvirate. Tremayll, a sergeant at law, then found himself at odds with Hody and had to go to law to defeat him.

There had been a house on the site in the 14th century and John Kenne, John's grandfather, had had a small chapel in it in 1417. This house was totally replaced by Tremayll (later Sir Thomas Tremayll) before his death in 1508. Blackmoor Farm, in local red sandstone rubble, comprises a main hall range of three rooms and a porch entry facing east, with a chapel wing coming forward at its north end. A slightly later kitchen wing runs back from its southern end. In both angles thus formed is a stair turret – that in the rear combined with a two-storeyed garderobe. The hall has a moulded framed ceiling, and the roof of the chamber above has arch-braced jointed crucks and windbraces. The chapel is clearly recognizable from its niches and piscina. The porch and the chapel gallery are probably additions of about 1600; from that time no significant alteration was made.

Thomas Tremayll, surely the builder of Blackmoor, died in 1508 still active as a lawyer in London and as a sheep farmer at Blackmoor. In his will he distributed his household goods, plate, stock and cash with an even hand among his family, carefully (as a lawyer surely

Below left. Blackmoor Farm, the hall.

Below. Blackmoor Farm. An upstairs bedroom showing the curved windbraces in the roof.

Blackmoor Farm. The east front with the porch and chapel.

would) noting featherbeds, bolsters, sheets, blankets, and silver mounted 'nut' cups. Concerned that he might possibly have taken money in the course of his professional life to which he was not entitled, he instructed his executors to give away five marks (£3.66p) to the poor, or more 'if it can be done'. And he noted in particular that there were goods at Blackmoor which had once belonged to William Dodesham, perhaps his old mentor. These, with other property, he directed should be sold for the benefit of Dodesham's soul.

Thomas's son John evidently thought himself dying in 1513, but finding it a false alarm he abandoned his first will, married again, and in November 1534 made another. This will and the accompanying inventory survive because his second wife, the widow of John Halswell of Goathurst, brought to Blackmoor her son Nicholas. Tremayll paid for his education in London as the inevitable lawyer and married him to his daughter. Will and inventory are still among the Halswell (later Kemeys-Tynte) family archives. The inventory lists the contents of the house at the time of John's death in 1535, arranged as the compiler walked at his task from room to room. So the house can be described: hall, parlour and buttery on the ground floor of the main range with great and parlour chambers above; oriel (perhaps, as at Lytes Cary, the west end of the chapel) and chapel in the north wing with the chapel chamber above; kitchen, larder, bakehouse and 'yeldynge' house in the rear wing with press and kitchen chambers over. The furnishings, Tremayll's clothes, cattle on the farm and the contents of the chapel – a chalice, vestments, four books and four tapestry cushions (cosshynges) – were valued at £119 2s.

The house on John's death was leased to Nicholas Halswell, and to him it eventually passed. Nicholas preferred his own ancestral home, now part of Halswell House in Goathurst, but it was obviously with the help of Tremayll's money that he was able to build a worthy home. The law again provided.

Halswell House

The reality of feudal connexions may long have passed when in 1565 Robert Halswell, heir to his late father Nicholas, was reminded by the Queen's escheator that he held his manor of Halswell from William Paulet, lord of the neighbouring manor of Goathurst. For Nicholas, at any rate, the notion might well have been irksome, for he had been a man of consequence; a lawyer involved in many deals for the sale of former monastic and chantry land, and then M.P. for the borough and port of Bridgwater. He was, too, a man with deep roots in his manor; in 1318 his ancestor William Halswell had influence enough to obtain licence from the bishop to have mass celebrated by his own chaplain in his own private chapel at a house called Halswell Court. Since that time Halswells had not exactly prospered, but they had at least persisted; whereas Nicholas's 'superior' at Goathurst had not achieved his eminence nor had his family survived for so long.

Perhaps there was little to choose between their two houses at the time: in fact, the plasterwork still surviving from the Goathurst manor house displays a style not found in the older parts of Halswell. Yet two centuries on and the grounds of the former had been encroached upon by new houses in the village street while the manor house itself was later to be adapted as the Rectory. Halswell manor at that same period, the 18th century, was a considerable and elegant mansion surrounded by landscaped gardens and park.

The mansion, of course, had modest beginnings. No part of the present building can be assigned to the time of William Halswell in the early 14th century, but behind the great north range of the present house are two more modest and irregular wings forming two sides of a courtyard, the earliest part of which may belong to the early 16th century. There are doorways with four-centred heads, one of which bears the letters N.H. for Nicholas Halswell, who, having been trained as a lawyer under the eye of his step-father John Tremayll of Blackmoor, used some of his inheritance in 1536 'for the building of his manor of Halswell'.

To Nicholas Halswell's prosperity his will and a schedule of his lands bear witness. Robert, his son, survived him by only six years and then came Nicholas, his grandson, in 1570 just over three years old, who inherited at once his father's gold chain and armour and the title deeds to his father's lands locked securely in a coffer in the parlour. The armour was presumably rather large for the lad,

Right. Halswell House from the park, showing the north front.

Below. Halswell House from the north-east in the late 18th century, showing the 'Temple on the lawn' built in 1755.

but the gift was, in a sense, symbolic. In later life Nicholas secured confirmation of his family arms and crest and was knighted. This Nicholas seems to have contributed little to the house – only a corridor is certainly his work, datable probably between 1595 and 1610, a period when several times he paid customs duty on imported freestone at the port of Bridgwater. He died in 1633 having fathered six sons and a daughter and outlived at least two of them including his eldest son. Henry, the second son, succeeded his father and was in turn succeeded in 1637 by his brother Hugh. Hugh was a clergyman and a reluctant squire who was content to pass his responsibilities through his only daughter Jane to her husband, Colonel John Tynte of Chelvey.

Some forty cavaliers with their servants and over a hundred horse, possibly once part of Lord Goring's unruly crew which had disintegrated at Langport, had temporary and free quarters at Halswell in July 1645. That was, perhaps, justice if Tynte was by then in possession, for he had been the so-called commander of a regiment of horse which earlier in the year had plundered at Axbridge, South Brent, Lympsham and Berrow. Tynte later claimed that he had resigned his command before the trouble, but it is clear that it was long before his actions for the King were forgiven. In a closet within his chamber at Halswell he kept his most intimate papers including his summons to Haberdashers Hall, a Protection issued by Lord Fairfax, his discharge out of prison in Taunton, and his pardon from Parliamentary commissions. Only in 1656 were the Major-Generals convinced of his loyalty.

The entrance to the north wing dated 1689, built for Sir Halswell Tynte, perhaps by William Taylor.

In 1667, when the boy reached the age of eighteen, Hugh Halswell settled his ancestral estate on his grandson, the son of his daughter Jane and John Tynte who had been tactfully christened Halswell. Thus began the Tynte ownership of Halswell which lasted until the 20th century.

In a letter now among the Thynne papers at Longleat William Taylor, a London surveyor, wrote in March 1683 that before he could return to London he was obliged to visit Sir William Portman, presumably at Orchard Portman, and then Sir Halswell. Tantalizingly there is no more, and Howard Colvin, knowing of the date 1689 over the entrance to the great north range at Halswell, commented that if Taylor's involvement could be substantiated, it would 'establish him as a designer of some importance'.

The design certainly fitted the owner. For his loyal service to the Royalist cause during the Civil War John Tynte had been one of the intended knights of the projected Order of the Royal Oak whose establishment was considered too divisive for safety. Not long after the death of his grandfather, Mr Halswell Tynte was in 1674 created a baronet, a proper recognition of loyalty as the son of a cavalier and the husband of a grand-daughter of Sir Beville Grenville. Sir Halswell served as sheriff of the county and four times as M.P. for Bridgwater. His new building was a statement in stone that the Tyntes had come to West Somerset; that Sir Halswell was a power which his ancestors had never been.

The family papers were scattered in 1950 but among those that are known to survive none contain any reference to the building of the great north range. Possibly based on French pattern books of the time rather than on English, it stands bold and tall, masking the older buildings from the visitor approaching along the drive. Three storeys high with a flat roof and balustrade, its seven-bay front has slightly projecting, two-bay wings, and in the centre is the main entrance, directly into the great hall. The round-headed doorway is set back in a curved niche flanked each side by two rusticated pillars and a classical quarter column. Above the niche, finely carved trophies occupy the spandrels. The central window immediately above and lighting a gallery or drawing room is a simple sash under a broken pediment in which a shield bears the family arms. The window is framed by panels with hanging garlands and ears of corn, and above the pediment is carved the date, 1689, in Roman numerals.

This imposing addition created the mansion which was home to Sir Halswell Tynte until his death in 1702 when he was succeeded by his son John, whose marriage to the eventual heiress of the Kemeys family of Cefn Mably (Glamorgan) was to bring a Welsh estate and other interests to the family. John died in 1710 and was followed by three of his sons in turn, two of whom died young without children. The third son, Sir Charles, who used the name Kemeys-Tynte, held Halswell from 1740 until his death in 1785. To him must be credited many minor works on the house: replacing wainscot in the parlour and using old material in the library chamber; putting sashes in the west range; hanging shutters in the Justice Room, installing a chimney piece and bookcases in the Library; rough casting the east front above the rusticated stucco; and reconstructing the west front of the house to the designs of Francis Cartwright of Blandford.

But Sir Charles' main concern was for his park and garden. He built a new garden and water house in 1750; a long lake and other ponds in the valley beside the house, a circle of trees and an avenue to west and south-west by 1756. In the late 1760s Sir Charles sent his agent specifications for building a hermit's house on a hill in the park and a temple in the wood, presumably the Temple of Harmony, which emerged from a design by Robert Adam in 1767 and was equipped for alfresco meals with a kitchen and a cupboard for china. The

A portrait of Sir Charles Kemeys-Tynte, the creator and probably designer of the park in the 18th century.

architect John Johnson exhibited drawings for a Temple of Pan in 1778, and had earlier designed and built the Riding School.

An inventory made on Sir Charles's death listed 71 rooms in the house, usually described by the style or colour of their decor — the little Chintz room, the Yellow Satin room — contrasting with the more mundane mangle room, laundry and so on. There were in the house portraits of royalty as befitted such a loyal family, including those of Charles I and Charles II; and among the plate were items such as a muffineer and a pair of asparagus tongs. The hothouses and greenhouses near the house ensured that the table at Halswell was exquisite. Sir Charles's widow held the estate in dower and meticulous records of her rule have survived. Lemons, oranges, citrons, myrtle, jasmine, coffee trees, pepper trees and prickly figs were among the exotics in the hothouses, and Lady Tynte collected melon seeds from the Dukes of Manchester and Marlborough and Mr Schutz to be planted in a prepared hotbed. The many ponds in the park in her time produced tench, carp and crayfish.

On Lady Tynte's death in 1798 Halswell passed to a niece, Jane Hassell, wife of Colonel John Johnson, who had taken the name Kemeys-Tynte. By that date the house was only occupied by servants; the plate was, in Hoare's Bank in London; the furniture was old-fashioned. Members of the family used Halswell occasionally, but visitors' picnic parties were often to be seen and even encouraged in the grounds. Charles Kemeys-Tynte, Jane's son, succeeded his mother in 1825 and twenty years later established his claim as heir to the Barony of Wharton. His great-grandson, Charles Theodore Halswell Kemeys-Tynte, succeeded as Lord Wharton in 1916.

Early in the morning of 27 October 1923 Lord Wharton's valet was awakened by smoke coming through the floor of his room at the top of the house. The Halswell fire hose was soon in action and villagers were quickly at work helping the butler to remove furniture and pictures. No fire brigade was available at Bridgwater or Taunton and the Glastonbury brigade, alerted by Lord Wharton's chauffeur,

Below. The neglected Temple of Harmony, designed by Thomas Prowse in 1764 and based on the temple of Fortuna Virilis in Rome. One of several temples in the park.

Below left. Robin Hood's Hut in 1900, originally built for Sir Charles Tynte in 1765 at a cost of £300, including a room called the Hermit's Room.

The east front, largely the work of lawyer Nicholas Halswell in the 16th century.

did not arrive until 7.15. By that time Sir Halswell Tynte's great north range was 'completely gutted'- ten bedrooms, the drawing room, reception hall, dining room. 'Practically all that remained of the front part of the building', declared the local newspaper, 'were the blackened outside walls, the interior being a mass of smouldering debris'. The smouldering went on for hours, and part of the west wall collapsed. Paintings by Vandyke, Hoppner and Gainsborough were destroyed, but the silver was untouched. The cause of the fire was later traced (after allegations of sabotage and arson in the National Press) to the newly-installed electricity supply. By that date the estate was heavily mortgaged but repairs and restoration were undertaken at an estimated contract cost of £41,534 10s, according to the plans of George and T.S.Vickery of Gresham Street by J.Long of Bath to a standard and accuracy which many have taken as the original workmanship.

The family returned to the restored mansion until the Second World War when a Prisoner of War camp was established in the grounds. The house and parkland were sold in 1950 and the house itself was divided into flats and used as a furniture store. The present owners of most of the house have undertaken the almost herculean task of restoring both the mansion and its grounds and to protect, in one case against wilful neglect, what remains of the park and its temples. Their vision has now been caught by others, and Halswell has, rather late, been recognized for what it is. In the words of Gervase Jackson-Stops it boasts 'perhaps the finest "undiscovered" garden of its period in England', and at its centre a mansion of great nobility.

Hinton House

Cosmo, Grand Duke of Tuscany, came to Hinton soon after 1660 and was impressed. 'Very different from the common style' was his verdict on a house which had been remarkably transformed over the previous quarter century by Somerset's leading Royalist family, the Pouletts. Part of that transformation had been achieved despite heavy fines imposed on the family for their activities on behalf of the King during the Civil War, a loyalty to the Crown which they had shown for more than a century.

About 1430 young William Paulet or Poulett, from Beere near Cannington, married Elizabeth Denebaud of Hinton and so began a line which lasted there until 1973. William himself is said to have died at a great age in 1488, leaving his son Amias to alter the old Denebaud house producing, as John Leland noted, 'a right goodly maner place of frestone, with 2 goodly high tourres embatelid in the inner court'. This house, comprising a hall, parlour, and service wing, still stands in the heart of the present mansion, and much more survived into the 18th century. Then its impressive courtyard frontage was still to be seen, its entrance porch flanked by three-storeyed bay windows and slender towers, partly, perhaps, the work of Amias's son Sir Hugh.

Amias was an interesting man, a solid gentleman of the type on whom the Tudor dynasty depended. Under suspicion for supporting the Duke of Buckingham against Richard III in 1483, Amias was attainted. He presumably escaped abroad, was appointed Henry Tudor's first sheriff of Somerset and Dorset while still under the age of thirty, and fought at the battle of Stoke, where he was knighted. In 1513 he was in command during an expedition in France, but a year or two later was in trouble. It seems that a young schoolmaster, appointed rector of Limington near Ilchester by his patron, came down to take up his duties and for some unknown cause was put in the stocks by the local magistrate. The magistrate was Sir Amias; the schoolmaster fifteen years later in 1515 was appointed Lord Chancellor of England — none other than Thomas Wolsey. Wolsey apparently never forgot the occasion, and summoned Poulett to London, putting him under house arrest in the Middle Temple for several years. There, it was said, Sir Amias erected a gatehouse which he decorated with cardinals' hats and other devices to flatter his erstwhile prisoner-turned-gaoler.

Amias's son Sir Hugh (died 1573) was in the same respectable

The tomb of Sir Amias Paulet and his wife in the family chapel in the parish church.

mould as his father — with the army in France in 1544, knight-marshal of Russell's forces which defeated the Western Rebellion in 1549, Captain and Governor of Jersey in 1550 and Vice-President of the Welsh Marches in 1559. Sir Hugh's son Amias (1536-88), puritan, diplomat and friend of Walsingham, had the unenviable task of acting as keeper of Mary, Queen of Scots, at Tutbury, Chartley and Fotheringhay. Neither he nor his son are known to have altered Hinton, but his grandson John's loyalty to the Crown received its due reward. At first a cavalry officer and later a student of the Middle Temple and M.P., his London life made Hinton seem 'a dull dirty place'. He was happy enough to entertain Charles I there in 1625 and for his treatment of a diplomatic prisoner and other services he was made Baron Poulett in 1627, much to the chagrin of his local political rival, Sir Robert Phelips of Montacute.

Active for the King from 1642 onwards, when his house was defended against the trained bands acting in the name of Parliament, he entertained his sovereign again at Hinton in 1644. He was taken prisoner at Exeter in 1646 and was heavily fined. He was to pay £1,500 compensation to Lady Drake for damaging her house, part of a total fine actually levied at £2,742 in addition to which his son, for his loyal service to the Crown in Ireland, had to find £3,760.

Within five years of what might have been a crippling blow, work was being done on the house which suggests remarkable powers of recovery. There is an account book recording spending in the years 1652-5 which refers to old parts of the house being altered, other parts described as new and perhaps completed not long before, and to work actually being undertaken. Old parts were the great hall, the oriel, the hall porch and a tower, the gallery, the little parlour, 'my Lady's closet' and the armoury. New by 1655 were a closet, stairs in the blue room, 'my Lord's chamber' and another hall, a chapel, and four courts — brewhouse, wash-house, stable and dairy. Not far away

Hinton House. The 'goodly maner place' of Sir Amias Paulet with its long 17th-century flanking wings, from an engraving dated 1791.

was the brick and freestone banqueting house on the bowling green on which the second Baron Poulett expended most of his money.

By 1664 the enormous number of 47 hearths were recorded in the house. There had clearly been a vast extension by the first baron before 1649 which was concluded by his son. The interpretation by John and Jane Penoyre, who have recently studied the house in detail, seems entirely reasonable: two long narrow, two-storeyed wings running west from the old house forming a forecourt, the northern one perhaps forming a link between a detached kitchen and the service rooms, the southern heading from the old parlour wing which was widened and extended east to form the great State Apartments whose south front is the remaining most impressive feature of the house and a direct parallel with the apartments at Brympton. One other Brympton parallel may be the new porch entrance, placed at Hinton centrally and its former position converted to an oriel. The rainwater heads on the south side of the State Apartments bear the arms of the first baron and his wife; and a bird in one plaster ceiling in

The 17th-century south range or State Apartments incorporating an earlier parlour at the west end behind the entrance front.

The monument to the 1st Baron Poulett (died 1649), courtier and royalist.

the dining room, itself a later copy, bears the date 1636. The north-west wing (and probably its fellow) seems to have been built by 1640.

The second baron's purse might have been much slimmer (and his political fortunes more straitened) had he not been married to the sister of Sir Thomas Fairfax's wife. John, the third baron, married an earl's daughter and served from 1674 until his death in 1679 as Lord Lieutenant of Somerset. His son, yet another John and born in 1663, was 'a very weak child' and 'so marvellous infirm of the king's evil [scrofula] that his life is under great suspicion (unless his present ague helps to lengthen it)'. The ague was efficacious: he lived to the age of eighty and was, despite his 'mean figure', described while still under thirty as 'certainly one of the hopfullest Gentlemen in England'. He was undoubtedly the most distinguished member of his family since the 16th century. In 1688 he was quick to give his support to William of Orange and allowed him to hunt in his park when he stopped at Hinton on his inexorable way from Brixham to Whitehall.

Lord Poulett's affection, however, was for Princess Anne. He served her as Privy Councillor for the whole of her reign, and in return she created him Earl Poulett in 1706. He was First Lord of the Treasury in 1710-11 and Lord Steward of the Household 1711-14. Her death brought his own political eclipse. Local lore for long ascribed the State Apartments to Inigo Jones who, it was said, designed them for a visit of the Queen to Hinton. The premise in untenable, though she may well have occupied rooms there; perhaps she came to stand sponsor to one of the earl's younger children who thereafter had to bear her name despite his undoubted male sex. Yet it seems likely that the earl modified those State Rooms, adding a grand staircase on the north side and possibly a chapel. He also built single-storeyed wings running north and south slightly detached from those forming the entrance courtyard.

Possibly Matthew Brettingham, at some date between 1747 and 1764, may have joined these wings to the main building and done some internal work. Much more extensive alterations in the Classical style were carried out probably between 1789 and 1793 by John, the fourth earl, who succeeded in 1788 and married money. According to the Duchess of Devonshire his bride had a great fortune, a 'comical ugly face', and a waist 'longer than her legs'. Presumably with the help of her money (and after her death he married a widow whose family were also Nabobs who had made large sums of money in India), the earl made sweeping changes, actually reducing the residential accommodation but vastly increasing the size and scope of ancillary rooms. The whole structure was changed both in style and proportion: in style Classical, the work of an otherwise unknown surveyor named Felton; in proportion by raising the level of the ground around the building (except before the State Apartments which retained the original level to form a sunken garden), thus emphasising width rather than height. At the same time the original house was almost entirely demolished: towered entrance front and hall disappeared, and in their place a symmetrical west front with a central, octagonal entrance and Grand Saloon at the new level. The south-west wing was also demolished, and behind the north-west wing was formed a new service court and estate office. East of that, still between house and village, rose a new stable court including coach house, riding school and billiard rooms.

Despite these radical changes, the fourth earl was not quite satisfied. Felton's work had created a Georgian house, but Sir John Soane was evidently commissioned to go further. The problem seems to have been the entrance, perhaps not impressive enough for so large a house. Soane suggested the rebuilding of the State Apartments with an entrance portico there. In the event these ideas were rejected, although Soane's preparatory drawings provided many clues to the work of Felton. Then enter James Wyatt (died 1813) and his nephew Sir Jeffrey Wyatville.

Wyatt remodelled the Grand Saloon in a Gothick style and turned the Georgian frontage into a Gothick facade with octagonal turrets. He built a corridor in the same style, its vaulted ceiling lit by coloured glass. A new staircase was built about 1804. Circulation within the house was thus improved and the facade was again the height of fashion. Wyatville then in a sense turned the whole house round. True, the facade and the south wing still looked across the vast park, but on the north side of the house he built a delightful *porte cochère*, almost a processional arch. The west range of the stable court was at the same time converted into a long grand entrance hall which brought visitors to an ante room, then to Wyatt's Gothick corridor, then to the Grand Saloon. Here was now a mansion fit for the man who was Somerset's Lord Lieutenant, Colonel of the Somerset Fencible Cavalry and of the East Somerset Militia, and a Lord of the Bedchamber in successive Tory administrations.

The building earl died in 1819 and was succeeded by his equally Tory son who voted against the Reform Bill, begat three sons who all died before him, and was succeeded by a nephew in 1864. William Henry, educated at Sandhurst, saw active service in Afghanistan and married three times, unsuitably. After his death in 1899 there followed a disputed succession which attracted the Press and cartoonists. One claimant, the late earl's son by the daughter of a Portsmouth pilot, called himself Viscount Hinton and was left £5,000 by the Duchess of Cleveland, a distant relative, to become a Ceylon tea planter. He died in Holborn workhouse in 1908. The successful claimant, William John Lydston, married a chorus girl from the Gaiety Theatre who had appeared on the stage from the age of six. The earl died in 1918 aged thirty-five, leaving as his heir George Amias Fitzwarine, eighth and last Earl Poulett, who sold the house and estate in 1958. He died in 1973.

The great park, created by William Kent and planted with such care, has now returned to agricultural use whence it came. A few of

The north-west range and the 'Gothick' west front, with the battlements and flag staff of the *porte cochère*.

the noble trees – American Clumps they were called – still stand, but purchasers of the house and grounds lacking Poulett discrimination re-sold for a quick profit. A more considerate owner in 1969 was prevented from restoring it by unsympathetic planning demands.

Every country house of this size was a community in itself, and the villagers over the wall or beyond the shrubbery were dependent upon it for their livelihood. In 1837 there were 21 indoor servants at Hinton, 10 gardeners and 3 gamekeepers. In 1856 17 indoor and outdoor male servants were assessed for taxes, and also assessed were 5 carriages, 8 horses, 2 ponies, 16 dogs, and 2 people who still wore hair powder (duty 23s 6d each). More than a century earlier, in 1725, food recorded in the kitchen book from 18-31 December cost £12 15s 2d and included 490 lbs of beef, 950 oysters, 270 eggs, 140 lbs of veal, snipe, larks, woodcocks, a partridge, 2 quails and a fieldfare, 1 cwt of salt, 30 lbs of mustard seed and 7 lbs of sugar. That was for feasting one family and its retainers. Today the house has been saved from destruction and decay. It is home to families who occupy not only those rooms originally designed for domestic oc-cupation but also the stables (called Brettingham Court) and the kitchen court (Wyatt Court), and even the *porte cochère*. It is a com-munity again, preserved and lived in probably not to the excess suggested by the kitchen book, but with enthusiasm by owners who appreciate what it is to live in a country house without the awesome responsibility of its total maintenance.

Lympsham Manor

One of the consequences of the English Reformation, the transfer of power and patronage from Church to State, was the creation of that apparent anomaly the lay rector, the landowner who, having purchased an estate formerly in monastic hands, found himself possessed of the duty to appoint parochial clergymen and also the owner of tithes and lands which in time past had been given for their support. Lympsham had been one of those places, anciently in the ownership of Glastonbury Abbey but transferred to secular hands when the abbey fell and from 1616 belonging to the Poulett family, later Barons and Earls Poulett of Hinton St George. The phrase lay rector was not used in their case; this would have confused their status still further since the clergyman at Lympsham was also styled rector. What the Pouletts possessed was land in the parish and the right to appoint the rector. The land was actually very close to the church, which had once belonged to Glastonbury. It was, perhaps, pretentious to call it a manor, but so it was; the owner had the right to hold courts to govern the estate just as did any other lord. The Pouletts did not, of course, need a house there – the land was hardly valuable enough for that, and in any case they had several other places in which to live.

This curious arrangement lasted until 1809 when John, fourth Earl Poulett, sold his interests in Lympsham to the Revd Joseph Adam Stephenson, one of a long line of almost hereditary Anglican clergymen whose father was vicar of Olney in Buckinghamshire but who traced his family back to Rawmarsh in Yorkshire where three generations had been rectors between 1666 and 1762. Joseph Adam had been educated at the Queen's College, Oxford, and came to Lympsham with funds inherited from the Stillington family of Kelfield and obvious religious zeal. His marriage in 1812 to Elizabeth Gurdon brought him two sons, the younger of whom was to follow him as rector and was to be the creator and sustainer of the 'sacred homestead' which so impressed a visitor in 1845.

That visitor, who preferred to be known as 'Churchgoer', was actually Joseph Leech, editor of the *Bristol Times*. He came to Lympsham on one of his regular Sunday sermon 'tastings' and described in detail the conduct of the service and the enthusiasm of the parishioners. He noted in passing on his way to church the schoolhouse and 'pretty parsonage' which stood together and seemed 'in their smiling contiguity and repose, one sacred

Lympsham Manor from the south-east showing the 1867 conservatory.

homestead'. 'The parsonage', he went on, 'is an exceedingly pleasing and picturesque object in the view, with its long front and its pretty porch, and its oriel windows . . . an air of elegance and competence beside so tempting, that were comfort all a man sought for in the ministry, there are few laymen . . . who would not be quite willing to exchange places with the rector of Lympsham'. Leech did not know the history of the parish, and he would certainly have commented, had he known, that the young rector he saw at the parsonage door was also a manorial lord. And yet he sensed what to some might have been an anomaly: here was a squarson indeed.

'Churchgoer' saw the second generation Stephenson. Joseph Adam had died in 1837 but had bequeathed to his parish a schoolroom, built in 1820, and to his son and heir a Gothick fantasy which was both parsonage and manor house. It is a simple building only in form, a long two-storeyed range of six bays, broken into sections of 3, 2 and 1 bays, the roof line falling slightly at each junction, the pierced parapets changing in pattern. The whole concept with decorated buttresses, string courses, shields, pinnacles and Tudor mullions creates a curious and unlikely unity out of a concoction of medieval styles. Gothic Revival in period, but ogee curves are not much in evidence and the window heads are of almost any form – trefoils under mullions here, lancets and double lancets under square or pointed drip moulds there. On the east side is a pinnacled and elaborately carved entrance; at its north end a little turret corbelled out from the first floor; at the south a conservatory, a pavilion in stone; and on the west two polygonal towers of three

An engraving of Lympsham church and Rectory c.1840, showing the original conservatory.

storeys and another two-storeyed bay. One tower contains a tiny chapel to which the rector could descend from his study via a trapdoor and ladder to address his family and staff.

The credit for this house belongs to Joseph Adam Stephenson and the date is 1814-15 according to the answers he gave to visitation questions from the bishop: there was no parsonage house in 1814, there was a house in 1815. Possibly his son added some of the details, certainly the conservatory in 1867. Its heavier mouldings are reminiscent of his other work on the estate. Joseph Adam may have built the blacksmith's house, for its more delicate windows contrast with the heavy mouldings of the forge itself.

'Churchgoer' was impressed by the parsonage grounds: 'no stiff walls about them; and a light rustic paling, or a wire fence, or a row of evergreens' divided the house from the village. So it remains: the house can still be glimpsed from the church through trees and shrubs, and curving drives from south and north provided two ways for traffic, from the north passing the Classical stables and coach house.. Joseph Henry added a lodge at the southern entrance, and to him must belong the wrought iron gates and arched brackets into the shrubberies and churchyard, the brackets once holding gas lamps.

Joseph Adam was the creator of the homestead but Joseph Henry, perhaps with more enthusiasm but a little less delicacy of taste, continued to build. He was still at Oxford when his father died in 1837, and so a 'conditional' rector was appointed to the parish; 'conditional' in that he was evidently prepared to yield the benefice when Joseph Henry should be properly qualified to hold it. Thus after a short curacy at Southport he came into his own, presenting himself to the bishop for institution in 1844. Here he remained until his death in 1901.

Joseph Henry's portrait in old age shows him a benevolent but formidable man. 'Churchgoer' had been impressed by him as a young man – natural eloquence (perhaps a little unrestrained, for the morn-

Prebendary Joseph Henry Stephenson, rector of Lympsham 1844-1901.

Lympsham Rectory from the west, c.1870, showing the tower containing the chapel and study from which Prebendary Stephenson descended via a trapdoor to address his family and staff.

The monument in Lympsham Manor garden to an Anglican and a Methodist, 1876.

ing sermon lasted an hour and a half), a kind, affectionate, friendly and earnest manner. Kindness and affection were the themes of his long ministry, and over the years local newspapers reported regular school treats, Christmas and tithe dinners at which the rector-squire entertained his parishioners. In return he accumulated handsome gifts from his grateful people in the form of illuminated addresses, silver gilt egg cups and silver inkstands.

Not all, of course, was done without criticism. The Methodists had a ranting campaign when he first came to the parish, but the joint memorial he erected to a Methodist and Anglican in 1876 in the parsonage grounds was an obvious example of his broad-minded approach. Trouble in 1858 led to fears that he might leave the parish, but on his return from holiday a gathering estimated at four thousand people, large quantities of food and flowers and a deputation from the Oddfellows so overwhelmed him that he declared he felt a very odd fellow indeed and there was no further talk of leaving. In the 1880s there was, perhaps, a little justification for feeling that the feasting in the parish was for the middle classes and not really for the poor, but such views were not widely held.

Yet when he contemplated the future, Joseph Henry (Prebendary of Dulcote in Wells Cathedral from 1856, Rural Dean of Axbridge from 1854, Diocesan Inspector of Schools 1845-79) must have faced a growing problem. He had sons to provide for and was fast outliving the time when parson and squire could comfortably be one and the same. In terms of actual income, his manor was worth in 1851 only £38 a year in comparison with his stipend as rector of well over £600. But he was still a landlord, responsible for tenants and their homes as well as for parishioners and their souls. Thus between 1863 and 1874 he built farms and cottages on his estate in his own distinctive style, a curious mixture of Victorian Gothic in rubble and freestone with polygonal brick chimneys and Tudoresque windows, each house bearing at least one sample of his coat of arms. The

church he had restored early in his time as rector. Thirty and more years later he built a combined school and parish hall, called Manor Hall, its main entrance carved with the text 'The Fear of the Lord is the beginning of Wisdom'. The children of Lympsham are still taught in Joseph Henry's school and still enter the yard through gates decorated with the letter S.

In 1872 when some of the large flat pastures in the parish were at last inclosed, Prebendary Stephenson changed the disposition of his estate. By exchanging fields he had bought as a private individual for fields belonging to the rectory manor which he held only as rector, he ensured that his family retained the house his father had built should none of his sons wish to take Holy Orders and follow him as rector. His plans were wise, although his own departure was long delayed. A foot damaged in childhood eventually made him so lame he was confined to a wheelchair from 1896, and for the same reason one of the first lifts in a private house was installed in the Manor. He died two days after Queen Victoria in January 1901, vastly mourned.

In a codicil to his will he left to his younger son the sum of £1,200 to build a new rectory house on condition that he should accept the living in his father's stead. Herbert Stephenson, with understandable trepidation in the face of his father's great achievements, took up the challenge until 1912 when he emigrated to Canada. His eldest brother Henry took up residence at the Manor on his father's death and was followed there by his son Bertrand, who in 1934 sold it to James Sydney Counsell. In a corner of the churchyard under the shelter of beech and sycamore Stephenson and Counsell lie side by side, sharing a piece of God's Acre as they had in turn occupied Lympsham's sacred homestead.

Above left. The entrance front, with its heraldic designs on the porch and oriel window.

Above. The Manor Hall, with 'S' design on the gates, built by Prebendary Stephenson as a parish school and hall.

Below. A rare survival: the exterior of the sand closet in the garden, and still in working order.

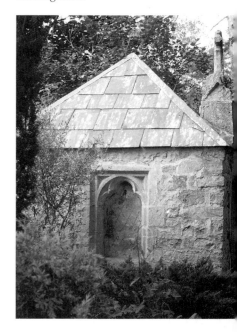

Lytes Cary

Philemon Holland's remark in his revised edition of Camden's *Britannia* that Lytes Cary was 'a place to be remembered' as the home of Thomas Lyte (died 1638) is but one of the attractions of a modest house set in the wide green plain of the Cary and the Yeo. For it is also a place to be remembered for a family whose almost obsessive record keeping has ensured that the various stages of the building of their house can be accurately dated.

That Thomas Lyte was more obsessed than the rest of his family resulted in the production of a commonplace book between the years 1611 and 1620. In it he noted family title deeds going back to Henry III's reign when his first ancestor William le Lyte (William the little) made his appearance. But there was much else including family property arrangements, notes on buildings and farming, recipes, and a mass of family letters as well as antiquarian notes made by his father, Henry Lyte, and himself. Some papers, Thomas noted, were 'in a square box by themselves', others 'in boxes inscribed on the outside'; 'in rolls in the great iron chest', 'in the great wicker hamper in the closet', 'in the great hamper', or 'in the window' in the closet. The great hamper contained 'unkind letters and worse dealings betwixt John Lyte esquire and his son and heir marked with a C'; there were other papers bearing on 'Mr Bellamyes unthriftye courses and willful fooleryes', the 'tyrannical dealings' of Henry Meer and the 'knaveryes' of Meer, Bellamy and another all against Henry Lyte and carefully preserved by Henry's son. The sale of Lytes Cary in 1755 inevitably brought about the dispersal and loss of this fascinating family collection, but the commonplace book survives, first studied in great detail by a Lyte descendant, Sir Henry Maxwell-Lyte who, as Deputy Keeper of the Public Records from 1886 to 1926, occupied a post for which his forebear Thomas Lyte was obviously so well fitted.

The family documents do not tell the beginning of the Lytes Cary story, but the appointment of a chaplain to a chantry there in 1343 is thought to mark the date of the earliest surviving building, the little chapel, once free standing but since the 15th century an integral part of the house. Its two-centred doorway, late Decorated windows and arch-braced roof with collar trusses clearly belongs to the mid 14th century, and the only older feature is the piscina, which may have come from an older chapel not far away.

The chapel was thus the work of Peter Lyte, who died in 1348 and was succeeded by his son Edmund, the first historian of the family.

A 19th century drawing by J. Buckler of the south range built by John and Edith Lyte c.1533.

Edmund died in 1418 and was followed by his son John and then by his grandson Thomas. One of those two must have rebuilt the old house, for the present hall and south-east range belong to the mid 15th century — witness the impressive roof of the hall with three tiers of delicately cusped windbraces, its arched braces supporting collar beams, and its finely carved wall plate. The other features to survive in the hall belong to the early 16th century and are the work of Thomas Lyte's son John.

John was born in 1498, studied law and in 1521 married Edith Horsey. According to his grandson, writing in the early 17th century, John 'newe buylt the Hall oriall, the 2 great portches, the closetts, the kitchen, and divers other places which are yet extant, with the dayrie house and the chamber over'. They are not all 'extant' now, but the porch and oriel on the east side of the hall are obviously John's work, and so, too, are the three-light windows, placed high to allow for wainscotting. The oriel, built out from the dais end of the hall, provided John and Edith with a private dining room approached through a low, panelled archway and made more comfortable with a fireplace. Over east porch and oriel were small

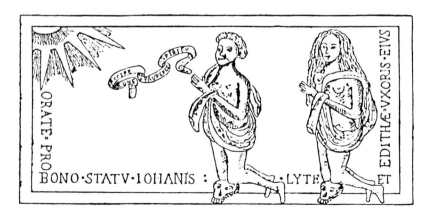

The curious picture of John (died 1566) and Edith Lyte, from the family pedigree.

chambers, perhaps the closets mentioned, both lit by bay windows resting on moulded corbels. Each chamber was topped by a gable crowned with a beast, a swan bearing the Lyte shield over the porch, and a griffin holding the Horsey shield over the oriel chamber.

There is now no trace of the second porch, the kitchen nor the dairy house and its chamber; but the south-east wing of the house, the solar wing, was quite obviously improved by John Lyte, for the magnificent bay window there bears the date 1533, the intials I and E for John and Edith, and the arms of Horsey and Lyte. The trefoiled crenellations each bear an heraldic symbol for the family's connexions: Stourton, Wadham and Fauntleroy as well as Horsey and Lyte yet again. The bay dominates the south front, which is otherwise lit by standard mullions. Inside, the wing is approached from the hall through a second panelled archway leading to a stair-case. In this range were rooms a respectable Tudor squire now found essential and which his 17th-century successors first panelled and later partitioned to provide by 1685 a great parlour in the centre, a chapel chamber forming the family pew to the east, and a little parlour and closet to the west. The Jacobean panelling is decorated at intervals with fluted Ionic pilasters. Above the great parlour is the great chamber whose rich coved plaster ceiling bears a ribbed geometrical design incorporating the arms of Lyte and Horsey and, on the east wall, the Tudor royal arms flanked by roses and lilies.

The Great Chamber in the south range before restoration, showing the plaster ceiling, heraldic devices, and panelled oriel. From a drawing by Sir R. Blomfield

How did John and Edith Lyte pay for all this new work ? The answer is partly by borrowing in 1537 the sum of £40 from the abbot of Glastonbury. John managed to repay £10 in January 1539 but the abbot sued for the remainder. John scraped together the rest at Midsummer and presented the abbot with £30 in gold angels during High Mass at the abbey when the abbot was in his private garden. Abbot Whiting returned eight angel nobles in return for a promise that John would 'sett upp the said Abbotte's armys in his new buldyng that he hadde made'. No such arms can now be found: the death of the abbot on Glastonbury Tor not many months later must have absolved John of his promise, or made its fulfillment rather dangerous.

One other contribution made by John and Edith but now no longer in the house is a series of at least 19 heraldic glass panels which probably adorned the windows in the south-east range. Very much in the Lyte genealogical tradition, they illustrate the alliances made by different members of the family down to John Lyte's own time. Some of these panels were later removed to the chapel. When the rest were disposed of is unknown, but Sir Henry Maxwell-Lyte discovered them in the church at Angersleigh near Taunton and removed them to his house in London. The family still owns them.

John Lyte, builder and family historian, died in London in 1566. He had already handed over much of the estate to his heir Henry, whose fame as a horticulturist is well known. Perhaps he was more successful in his chosen sphere than in maintaining his inheritance, if the papers mentioned by his son are any guide. *Lyte's Herbal*, published in 1578, was actually a translation from French of a Dutch work by Rembert Dodoens, first published in Antwerp in 1554. Lyte added some local material of his own, partly collected from the work of Dean William Turner of Wells. The book was a great success, and among his own papers were some of its practical applications: recipes for aromatic water, pomanders, perfumes and washing balls, and 'physicke notes good for the new sweat and other good old physike'.

Henry Lyte evidently established a botanical garden which had sixty different kinds of apple, over ninety types of pear, fifteen of plum. The pears have fascinating names showing their origins in all parts of England – Norwich, Kent and Windsor as well as Somerton and Cary Bridge. Also in the garden were specimens of almond, fig, quince, sloe, filbert and Cornish berry.

After the *Herbal* Henry turned his attention to genealogy, producing a book called *The Light of Britayne* which, by comparing proper names, proved to his own satisfaction that the British were descended from the Trojans. He went on, in another work, to show how the Lytes could also trace their ancestry to Troy.

Rather more scholarly work came from Henry's son Thomas, to whom the house and estate passed in 1607. In 1610 he presented to the king at Whitehall a genealogical table of the royal family entitled

The Great Hall and screen with angel-supported roof.

Henry Lyte the herbalist (died 1607) from the family pedigree.

'Brittaine's Monarchy', written 'on vellum with his own hand fairer than any print', illustrating a story stretching, not uncritically, back to Brutus. Thomas's reward was the gift of a portrait of the king himself and the Lyte Jewel, which he is shown wearing in his own portrait. Thomas also produced two magnificent genealogies 'not for any ostentation of birth or kinred . . . but only that those that are soe lately discended of on parentage and from on famelye might not be strangers on to an other'.

Thomas Lyte's contribution to his home was in the same vein, the repair, re-decoration and furnishing of the chapel in 1631. His work included a series of shields painted below the wallplate illustrating his family connexions: the more honourable on the east side, the rather less honourable on the north, the ladies on the south.

For a century after Thomas's death in 1638 Lytes remained prosperous enough, but another Thomas, great-grandson of the genealogist, found himself in financial difficulties and had to convey part of the manor and estate to trustees in return for an annuity. In 1748 his son sold the remaining Lyte interest and in 1755 it passed to Thomas Lockyer of Ilchester.

The house was considerably altered by Lockyer after 1770. The kitchen and other service rooms on the north-east were replaced by a farmhouse of two storeys, curiously dwarfing the medieval hall. Under part of the house is a vaulted cellar, possibly built by John Lyte in the earlier 16th century. Perhaps at the same time buildings on the west side of the courtyard were demolished, leaving the new house as the dwelling of a tenant farmer. Such a demotion of a fine house, unlikely at the time, secured the survival of the medieval buildings. When Sir Walter Jenner bought the property in 1907 the great parlour was a farm store, its panelling protected by layers of paint. The little parlour was a carpenter's shop.

Thomas Lyte (died 1638) wearing the jewel presented to him in 1610 by King James I.

A drawing by Benjamin Ferrey of the east front in 1841.

The east front, with the chapel, oriel, hall and 18th-century farmhouse wing sheltering behind topiary.

Over a period of forty years Jenner restored the house. He built the west wing to complete the courtyard and furnished it with pieces of great quality, producing a home of which John Lyte the builder would have been proud. At his death in 1948 the house and much of his furniture (including a bed in which Chatham may well have slept at Burton Pynsent) passed to the National Trust.

One of Sir Walter's great achievements was the formal garden which sets the house off to perfection. The grey lias of the walling and the golden Ham stone of the detailing are a perfect foil for the lawns and the topiary of which Henry Lyte the herbalist would undoubtedly have approved. Henry's garden was not the first here. In 1557 there arrived at Lytes Cary one Barnard Dovell of Old Cleeve and his daughter-in-law Grace. He had been allowed out of Ilchester gaol on bail after he had been arraigned for a serious affray near Cleeve Abbey. John Lyte had agreed to house him and his family at the request of Lord Thomas Howard, but when Dovell died while in Lyte's custody, more than a little problem arose. Dovell's friends claimed he had died of wounds received during the fight which had not been properly treated; others said he had been quite fit and well. John Lyte told how Dovell had walked to church, to Ilchester and to Somerton several times, played bowls and tennis in the grounds, caught perch with an arrow, quarrelled over the supper table with Sir John Wyndham, and actually died of the 'new sweat', refusing his hosts' attempts to care for him.

Marston House

That Marston House still stands is due in great measure to an historian, Michael McGarvie, who demonstrated to those who make such decisions that its destruction would be a loss of the greatest significance. For demolition seemed in the early 1970s to be the logical culmination of thirty years of damage and neglect. Memories still linger of a tented encampment in the park where the bedraggled and largely unarmed remnants of the British Expeditionary Force came to rest and recover after Dunkirk. Not long ago Nissen huts were still to be seen, reminders of the permanence of the temporary accommodation in war-time. And not long ago the physical ravages of the occupation of the house itself still left deep scars. But then, according to most of the guide books whose authors should have been better informed, the house was of no great architectural merit. Now the widely scattered records of the great family who loved it have been traced and induced to yield a different story; and a local businessman, in adapting the house as the headquarters of his world-wide quarrying interests, began the enormous task of restoration which his widow is determined to complete.

Marston Bigot was probably named after lakes which the river Frome often made in the clay valley and after a junior branch of the great Bigod family of Norfolk and South Wales. A succession of owners in the Middle Ages included the Stourtons who lived beyond the ridge to the south where lie both the Wiltshire village of Stourton and the Somerset priory of Stavordale, to which they had an attachment. Ownership thereafter is not easy to trace; a John Syms held it early in the 17th century followed before 1641 by Sir John Hippisley. This uncertainty comes at a crucial time, for at some date between 1600, when Marston manor-house was either on its old moated site in the valley or somewhere nearby, and 1641 a new mansion was built at the northern end of the parish, on the southern slope of the ridge called East Hill. 'A fair house', Lord Corke told his steward, 'with orchards, gardens, and pleasant walks about it', evidently by then all well established. The cost of house and land was £10,350, the purchaser Richard Boyle, created in 1620 Viscount of Dungarvan and Earl of the County of Corke in the peerage of Ireland, and from 1629 until his death in 1643 Lord High Treasurer of Ireland. By birth from Faversham in Kent, he had emigrated to Ireland in 1588 where, after some years facing financial problems, he was able to buy Sir Walter Raleigh's

Opposite top. A 'bird's eye' view of the early 17th-century house bought by Richard Boyle, the 'Great' Earl of Corke, in 1641, and remodelled by Lord Dungarvan in the 18th century.

Opposite bottom. The great south front, the central core flanked by offices to the right and the Ballroom and Conservatory to the left.

vast estate for a trifling sum and thus was able to create the basis for his fortune.

The purchase of Marston was made by a man known as the 'Great Earl' for his fair acquisitions of land and his public and charitable works in Ireland. He bought it for his fifth but third surviving son Roger, himself named 'the Wise'. Presumably before that wisdom became apparent he was at the age of six created Lord Boyle, Baron of Broghill, in 1628. What exactly was the house which had been bought in the young man's name, the house which he and his wife would call their English home ? Michael McGarvie recognised, and later restoration has revealed, that the house so many observers had dismissed conceals at its core a substantial Jacobean mansion which now forms the central portion of the present building. It was a house of seven bays with two-bayed wings coming forward at each end and a one-bayed stair wing occupying each angle. The central five bays were of three storeys and attics with a central pedimented door reached by semi-circular steps. The stairs ran through three storeys. The whole recessed centre was reached from a central, raised court-yard. The wings were of four storeys − three and basement − lit by windows which were probably transomed. The question of the designer may never be settled: tempting as it may be to suggest John Smythson by comparing Marston's form with that of Ham House in Surrey, the notion cannot, at least at present, be proved.

A corner of the restored library.

When the 'Great Earl' died in 1643 Roger, Lord Boyle of Broghill, became the owner of Marston. His Irish interests kept him from permanent residence here, but on the death of Charles I in 1649 he and his better-known youngest brother, the philosopher Robert Boyle, seem to have found it a safe haven at such a difficult time. Lord Boyle was in 1660 created Earl of Orrery and returned to a leading position in Ireland where he became President of Munster as well as a member of the English Parliament. At his death in 1679 Marston passed to his widow and for more than thirty years it remained an outpost of the Boyle estates, settled on the widows of three successive earls. The last died in 1713 and the property then reverted to Charles Boyle, the fourth earl of Orrery, a man who made Marston his home after the loss of his family seat in Ireland and the end of his diplomatic career as one of the negotiators of the Treaty of Utrecht. In 1711 he was created Baron Boyle of Marston and proof of his settlement in the county was his appointment in 1714 as Lord Lieutenant of Somerset, the first but not the last member of his family to hold the office.

Further proof of his interest in Marston was that before 1726 he had added a wing 'to complete the fabric' and in so doing 'enlarged the house within and rendered the building uniform and regular without'. And the house so improved was to be placed in fitting surroundings. By 1724 Stephen Switzer had begun to transform East Hill, work which he continued for the new earl between 1731 and 1749. During that period he built cascades, two ornamental pools in front of the house and behind, up the slope, a tree-lined avenue, lawns and shrubberies criss-crossed with paths in 'natural' or geometrical layouts. The whole was walled in the Baroque style. Also near the house was the parish church, two other buildings which might have been barns and stables, and an enclosure divided into regular cultivated plots.

Some time after succeeding in 1731 John, fifth Earl of Orrery, transformed his father's old-fashioned house. As befitted a cousin of the earl of Burlington who had made the Palladian style so popular, Lord Orrery's aim was to clothe the old in the outward appearance of the new, adding where necessary to provide 'the beauty of symmetry and order', which so appealed to Lord Burlington. In this work there is much clearer evidence of the identity of the designer: 'the plans were approved of or designed by Lord Dungarvan whose genius very much inclined towards architecture'.

This Lord Dungarvan was Charles Boyle, eldest son of Earl John, who was known by the title after his father succeeded his cousin in 1753 and became also Earl of Corke. The reference to his involvement comes from a 'narrative' of events at Marston written in retrospect by his step-mother Margaret, Countess of Corke, but there is no reason to doubt that the improvements were not carried out largely during the period when he was known by that title, namely from 1753 until his early death in 1759. The countess was in no doubt of Dungarvan's involvement in the alterations, which seem to have begun in 1749 and continued for some three years. This work involved the removal of the high gabled roofs, to be replaced by mansards behind balustrades; the replacement of the old transomed windows by large sashes with Gibbs surrounds; and further embellishments in the gardens. The interior was, of course, furnished with ornamental features so necessary at the time: statues, bronzes, busts and 'all kinds of useful and ornamental furniture'. Lord Dungarvan did not live long to enjoy the fruits of his efforts, and his father's financial difficulties seem often to have kept him away from the house he thought 'dear and delightful'. He died in 1762 still aged only fifty-five.

Two sons followed in quick succession, the elder dying in 1764. Edmund, Earl of Corke and Orrery, possessor between that date and his death in 1798, transformed the house again in the late 1770s by adding wings to east and west to the designs of Samuel Wyatt. The date on a rainwater head there is 1776. The eastern wing included the kitchens and service rooms which today house the communications centre of Foster Yeoman's international operations. The west wing was originally for stables and coach houses, together with the Library. Earl Edmund probably devoted little time to Marston despite all this expenditure. His life, so a contemporary wrote, was 'devoted to the most wretched voluptuousness' and he spent much time in Bath.

The next earl, also Edmund, succeeded in 1798. He was the first of

The great staircase.

Marston House in 1845.

his family to sign his name 'Cork' instead of 'Corke'. A professional soldier for a quarter of a century who saw active service against the French in Holland and Egypt, he turned his attention to Marston as soon as the war was over. His additions and alterations were radical: inside, remodelling rooms, forming passages, improving the proportions of the drawing room and some new service rooms. Changes outside were far greater. About 1817 a loggia of Ionic columns linking the two former Jacobean wings was added, probably to the designs of Sir Jeffrey Wyatville. More radical still, and probably again by Wyatville, was the diversion of the public road from in front of the house, where it also passed the old parish church, to the top of the ridge above East Hill. In its place a large terrace was created in the front of the long house – the original block and its additional wings. The basement floor was now buried, the front door brought to ground level. This work was complete by 1822. A print published in that year shows that Switzer's formal garden had been replaced by a much more informal landscape of lawns and trees. Perhaps this was the kind of landscape which most appealed to Lady Cork who, according to Mrs Bagot, 'used to sit in a green arbour which was all lighted up, dressed entirely in white, and looking like an old fairy'.

Richard Edmund St Lawrence, the ninth earl, came into possession of Marston at the age of twenty-seven when his grandfather died in 1856. The house was 'in a deplorable state of repair' and the estate in not much better case. The new earl could afford to be lavish, for his marriage had brought him a fortune. His wife, Emily Charlotte, was the daughter of the wealthy Marquess of Clanricarde and was herself 'pretty, clever . . . very well read . . . a brilliant talker'. Lord

The south front.

Cork, local Liberal M.P. until he succeeded his grandfather, was Lord Lieutenant of Somerset from 1864 until his death in 1904 and a Privy Councillor. In his time Marston became the glittering centre of county society.

Almost immediately on succeeding, Lord Cork commissioned C.E. Davis of Bath to design an entrance hall on the north side of the house with a grand staircase leading to new bedrooms. This addition is perhaps the most dignified and impressive part of the house, the part most seriously damaged by the wartime occupiers but now most carefully restored. This work was completed in 1858 and ten years later, after a new entrance drive had been made through the woods from the north-east, the west wing was reconstructed to include a ballroom and a billiard room. A huge laundry, replacement stables and finally a magnificent conservatory were added. The ballroom included a superb 18th-century marble chimney-piece from elsewhere in the house and a fine ceiling.

At the time of Lord Cork's death in 1904 house and estate were in splendid order but his heir, perhaps in financial difficulty and not caring for Marston as his father had done, divided the land and sold the house and contents in 1905. The house was sold again in the same year to the Bonham-Christie family, from whom it was requisitioned during the War.

House, estate and contents can never again be reunited, and decay has ensured that in some parts restoration is impossible. Yet the house is clearly emerging to life and beauty and usefulness again, and the hospitality which the present owner combines with business acumen will ensure that the mistakes of the Boyles will not be repeated.

Montacute House

The ornate forecourt wall and the house from the south east.

'A very faire yellow freestone house' was how Montacute was described in the later 17th century. The yellow has now weathered to brown, the freestone mellowed and is mottled with lichen. The house has long outgrown any suggestion that it stands as a brash gesture of defiance by some parvenu whose home turns dismissively away from Montacute village. Indeed, the Phelipses had owned property in the village in 1479, and great-grandfather Thomas, dying in 1501, had evidently been prosperous enough to request burial in the priory church rather than take his natural place with his neighbours in the parish church. And grandfather Richard Phelips and great uncle Thomas had sought careers in Dorset rather than in Somerset. But father Thomas had established himself modestly in Montacute, becoming in later life a querulous and compulsive letter-writer whose grammar and construction often successfully mask the message he was trying to convey. Yet in one of his clearer epistles he described an argument with a neighbour, who followed him through his house — through the hall, the court, the parlour, up the narrow and dark staircase to the parlour chamber. That was the house which he conveyed in 1587 to his fourth son Edward. Edward, by then established in London in the Law, had both wider horizons than his father and the means with which, on the rather narrow confines of his family holding, he could build the finest Renaissance mansion in Somerset; a house, indeed, to rival in a restrained English way the chateaux of the Loire.

The date 1588, it used to be claimed, could be seen somewhere in the house; 1598 is in a stained glass window; 1599 on the plaster overmantel, removed to the Buttery when it became a dining room in 1787; 1601 over the east doorway, perhaps marking the completion of the enterprise. No direct evidence of the designer has survived, no accounts of the building; but Dorothy Wadham later told her brother that Sir Edward Phelips had 'commended' a mason named William Arnold to her attention, and he was to be actively involved as chief craftsman if not designer of Dorothy's college at Oxford between 1610 and 1613. It has thus been assumed that Arnold, who worked for the Earl of Salisbury at Cranborne just before his Oxford contract and who was later to turn Dunster from castle to dwelling house, was responsible for Montacute rather earlier in his career.

He came, like many of his kind, with a pedigree, probably the son

of one Arnold Goverson (he himself was also known as William Goverson) who had worked as a joiner at Longleat in 1555. And was his more distant forebear that Arnold Craftman who in 1476 leased a quarry on Ham Hill? William himself came not as architect but as designer-stone mason, one of a school of West Country craftsmen whose products – chimney pieces, overmantels, porches, screens, mouldings, friezes – are to be found over a wide area, perhaps, like windows and doorways, to be bought from store or made to order at Ham Hill or some other quarry. Curiously, William lived for much of his life at Charlton Musgrove, not very near any notable quarry, although not very far from Montacute.

One hand may have directed the work, but Montacute is the product of different influences. The east front, almost more glass than wall, combines Classical details – entablatures between floors, the Nine Worthies, shell-headed niches, pedimented windows, obelisks on the balustrades – with Flemish gables and plain, rather severe transomed windows. All this decorating a main range of eleven bays with three-storeyed central porch, and two long wings at each end, forming the common 'E' frontage. Still in the later 17th century this frontage faced a formal terraced walk and then a court with a central stone pathway whose form but faintly echoed the medieval

Above. The great east front and forecourt.

Right. A pastoral engraving of Montacute House, together with the canal, park and St Michael's Hill in 1787.

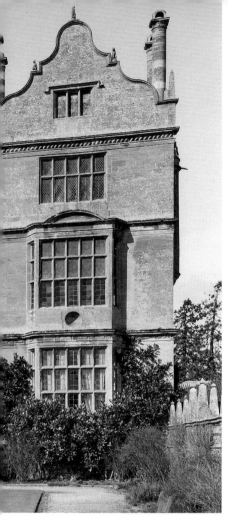

defended courtyard. Wall turrets became fantastical 'turrets of orna-
ment', corner bastions were transformed into delicate, square, two-
storeyed pavilions ('fair turrets with lodging chambers'), each face
bowed in the centre, decorated with obelisks and a Flemish parapet,
the ogee roof topped by a two-ringed finial. Obelisks and not men-
at-arms stand sentinel along the low balustraded walls to the central
gate with finialed piers, the rather less formidable defender of the
house than the 'fair gatehouse with lodging chambers' which stood
there in the 1660s, the whole simply dividing formal garden from the
park beyond.

That is the east front. The other sides of the house were all plainer,
the west front still symmetrical but with staircases broadening both
advancing wings and blank gables masking chimney breasts. The
plain symmetry of the north and south sides is wonderfully embellished by the dramatic, semi-circular oriels lighting the Long Gallery,
each oriel with 24 lights.

This was the 'very fair yellow freestone house . . . with a fair hall,
great and little parlour wainscotted, a dining room and withdrawing
room, and very many fair lodging chambers . . . and a fair gallery . . .
with divers good lodging chambers adjoining . . . and all other necessary rooms . . . very large and faire' which, it was believed when the
description was written in 1667, cost at least £20,000.

Designed by William Arnold or not, there is no doubt that the cost
was borne by Sir Edward Phelips whose portrait, painted towards the
end of his life, shows the symbols of office and social status, the mace
to signify his service as 'the worthy and judicious' Speaker of the

House of Commons 1604-11, and the arms in the window behind him to declare his gentle class. In 1611 he was appointed Master of the Rolls, a fitting climax to a legal career in which he took part in the trials of both Sir Walter Raleigh and Guy Fawkes.

Sir Edward's son Sir Robert followed his father's parliamentary career but crowned it not with royal approbation but rather as an able and effective opponent of royal privilege. He spent some months in the Tower but returned to the Commons to lead Members to produce the Petition of Right in 1628. His surviving letters, written in an almost illegible hand, reveal his varying attitudes to the crises of his times, leading the opposition in the county to Ship Money in 1635 and making Montacute a focus of County in opposition to the Pouletts of Hinton, the local champions of the Court faction.

Robert's sons Edward and Robert, however, both fought as colonels for the King during the Civil War, and the sale of tapestries from the house may have come about either to raise funds for the cause or to pay the fine imposed on Edward when he left the royalists in 1646. Sir Edward Phelips, who moved into the mansion when his father went to live in the farmhouse created out of the former priory buildings, was strictly loyal to the Crown in Charles II's time, and it is significant that no-one from Montacute joined the Monmouth rebels despite what happened in nearby villages. Yet his loyalty did not bring him wealth nor yet the title the Pouletts had achieved. Indeed, it seems that the family were already finding the great mansion hard to maintain. Sir Edward's successor, yet another Edward (1678-1734), had to marry his uncle's two daughters in turn to ensure that the estate was not hopelessly fragmented. Yet for some years his sacrifice was not rewarded: his aunt-and-mother-in-law persisted in survival. The best room in the house was said to be cluttered with lumber and much of the rest in 'mean condition'.

The next Edward probably saved the house, thanks in part to fortunate legacies. With his newly-acquired wealth he built a new west drive (1785-6) and in the recess between the two wings of the west side of the house he constructed a facade from the porch, pillars and other carved stone which had been part of a wing of Clifton Maybank House, Dorset, in origin older than Montacute but in the same golden Ham stone, and a house which had once been the home of Edith Phelips, aunt of Montacute's builder. Thus Montacute acquired a new aspect and at the same time increased convenience, for behind the new facade corridors were created for ease of access to the principal rooms.

That was, sadly, the end of the grandeur. The Phelipses, modest county squires rather than acquisitive country landowners, found they had not the means to maintain the great mansion. John Phelips, owner between 1806 and 1834, is said to have restored the house, but he may well have damaged the roof in his attempt to improve the Long Gallery. He is reputed to have been fond of giving parties

The 16th-century addition to the west front, brought from Clifton Maybank in Dorset in the 1780s by Edward Phelips.

and is remembered for his care for the unemployed in the neighbour-hood. Yet this caring man must have been sad that he had no children to share his musical and scientific interests, and when he died the furnishings of the house put under the hammer included four pianos, an organ and a harp, a theodolite, a telescope and the contents of the wine cellar.

The house stood empty for more than ten years until John's nephew William brought his bride there in 1845. Much work was contemplated by the young couple but, in some ways fortunately, very little was done. The ceilings in the Library and Long Gallery and some panelling and plaster work in the bedrooms, all in the popular Elizabethan Revival style and totally in keeping with the house, were added between 1845 and 1852, but perhaps a straitened purse prevented the planned addition of a massive service wing which some unknown architect proposed. He perhaps had his way with the south lodge and the stable block. From the late 1850s William Phelips's mental health prevented further changes, and in 1875 his son William Robert took over management of the estate, which in the agricultural depresssion of the time could not possibly have supported the house and family.

On the surface all was as it had ever been. When William Robert

The Library, formerly the Great Chamber, with its plaster overmantel and heraldic glass.

returned from Hampshire with his bride, Cicely Fane, in 1875 there was a triumphal arch over the west gate, their carriage was drawn by tenants down the drive to the front door, and dinners, treats, teas and dances were held in the village for a week. Christmas was also kept up in the traditional way: festoons of holly and ivy across the hall and other rooms, rituals of present-giving, carol-singing and attending church. But it was a cold house: there were hot pipes only on the ground floor and only one bath. Joyce Carew, Cicely's niece, remembered as a child not only the decorations but the intense cold, light only from flickering oil lamps, the enormous Christmas tree and the childrens' dance.

That same small girl clearly remembered other times – football in the Long Gallery with her cousins, the figure of old Mrs Phelips, widow of William, who occupied her own apartments in the Great Chamber, and who always headed the procession in to dinner, 'a tiny little figure with snow white hair covered by a pointed cap and very wisely – covered . . . with cosy shawls'. And at dinner she remembered the fountain supplied from a well under the dining table, the spraying water reflecting the bright colours worn by the guests.

The same cousin, growing up, stayed for the Montacute shooting parties and was a reluctant audience as 'Uncle Willie' discoursed on the iniquities of the Liberal government. There was still no heat and light in the house. The sale of family silver and pictures in 1895 was no permanent answer to the problem, and in 1911 W.R. Phelips had to leave. The house was first leased in that year; the last substantial farm was sold in 1918. By that time there was a new and rather dissatisfied tenant, George Nathaniel, Earl Curzon of Kedleston and Viscount Scarsdale, sometime Viceroy of India and (ironically enough) a member of the War Cabinet led by the man whose policies had driven the Phelipses from their home. Curzon, later Foreign Secretary and a leader of the Conservative Party, installed electricity and allowed his devoted admirer and mistress Elinor Glyn to redecorate the house. His bath, coyly hidden within a panelled cupboard, is the most memorable survival of his reign.

Curzon, who apparently waited on tenterhooks at Montacute after the resignation of Bonar Law to be summoned by the King, was bitterly disappointed to find that Stanley Baldwin had been preferred to his undoubtedly superior person. He died in 1925 and the Phelipses were faced with the disposal of the house. Gerard Almarus Phelips, from 1928 head of the family, assumed in the following year that it had been sold to Lord Waring. Whatever the difficulty, the house was finally disposed of in a much more acceptable way in 1931 through the generosity of Mr E. E. Cook's bequest to the Society for the Protection of Ancient Buildings. It was indeed fortunate that the society's secretary at that time was A.R. Powys, who had grown up at Montacute Vicarage and had been well acquainted with the Phelipses from childhood. The society presented the house to the National Trust.

The garden complements the house to perfection. The 1677 survey speaks of a walled area to the north with 'all sorts of flowers and fruit and divers mounted walks', a freestone banqueting house, and further walks and orchards. To the east beyond the gatehouse were more walks, rows of trees, and a bowling green. To the south, beyond the services and yard, were plums, pears, apples, cherries, two fishponds and the kitchen garden. To the west were elms and walnuts, a hop garden and stables. A century later the north garden was the 'best', with walks and a pond, but perhaps the glory had by then somewhat departed. The fashion was less for formality; the east forecourt, bereft of its gatehouse, led the eye directly to the avenue in the park.

The present garden was replanted for William Phelips in the 1840s and 1850s by Mr Pridham, whom Edith Phelips (née Helyar) had brought from her home at Coker Court. The orangery was built in 1848 and bears the ubiquitous obelisks. The borders, with strong colours and massed foliage, notably in the forecourt, leave a lasting memory of Montacute. Another will be the Long Gallery, now no longer a football field but home since 1975 to an exhibition of portraits of prominent men and women, many of whom would have known the creator of Montacute when he practised in the Law and busied himself in politics and government under Queen Elizabeth and King James I.

The north garden and Orangery, the 'best' garden with walks and a pond in the 18th century.

Newton Park

The four storey late 13th or early 14th century keep.

'A faire maner place like a castelle building' was how John Leland described the house in 1540 when it was among the several possessions of George Hastings, first Earl of Huntingdon. Botreaux, Hungerford and Hastings had held it in succession since 1375, as they had held North Cadbury, here succeeding the St Loes who had given their name to the place. The mansion built by the Langton family in the 18th century rejected ancestral antique in favour of elegance and taste. The old house was left isolated, then largely demolished to make way for a gravelled drive by which 'Capability' Brown, the creator of the park, proposed to lead Mr Langton's guests around his upper pond. All that now survives of the house has its own defence against further devastation in the unlikely form of modern buildings of the college which has occupied mansion and park since the Second World War and which now goes under the name of the Bath College of Higher Education Corporation.

Yet what survives comes as a great surprise: a gatehouse and a so-called keep. Excavations carried out by C. J. Arnold between 1975 and 1979 suggest some use of the site in the 12th and 13th centuries, but indicate the first substantial house there in the late 13th or early 14th centuries when two ranges were built forming an L shape, with a four-storeyed tower or keep in the angle. The outline of a spiral stair shows that the ranges were at least two-storeyed and that the tower was an independent unit with its own entrance and stair as well as a garderobe. Each room in the tower was presumably lit by narrow splayed windows like that surviving on the ground floor. The mullioned and transomed windows with arched lights of the upper floors belong to more domestic use in the 16th century. The crenellations may well have been a conscious attempt at picturesque for those 18th-century guests taking the air in the park. The worn coats of arms on the parapet are, however, genuine enough – St Loe and Botreaux, in their turn builders of the keep and of the two-storeyed gatehouse to the north-west.

This gatehouse is a gem, a vaulted tunnel with finely carved bosses at the intersections of the ribs. To the north is an open arcade, to the south a chamber. The entrance was defended with portcullis and gunloop and the original doors still survive. This building, too, was given turrets and crenellations in the 18th century.

Excavations were hampered both by the proximity of modern buildings and by the depth of rubble which overlies the site, but

Above. The gatehouse of the medieval manor.

Left. The fine ribbed vault of the gatehouse.

something of the truth of Leland's description was revealed, for he declared it to have been 'sumtyme one of the chief houses of the Lordes Sainct Lo', and the discovery north of the keep of a second tower, apparently at the other end of the long range attached to the keep, suggests the possibility of an east-facing range with towers at each end and protruding wings forming a courtyard entered by the gatehouse in its western side.

The original builder will probably never be identified but it must have been one of a succession of Sir John St Loes: perhaps the one who served at Acre with the future Edward I in 1271 and died in 1280, or his son who fought under the same commander in Scotland in 1299 and died in 1314. And perhaps the gatehouse was the work of Robert, Lord Hungerford, who presumably succeeded through his wife on the death of her father, William, Lord Botreaux, in 1462. This fortified house survived for Leland to see, but the Hastings owners were evidently little concerned with it as a dwelling for themselves and alterations may simply have been made for tenants. The Hastings estate rental of Newton was £53 10s 1d about 1560, and £29 13s 4d without the park about 1600. In the discrepancy lies the fact that in 1565 a property called the manor and actually meaning the demesne holding, the manor house and park, were sold to Edward Neville, the same who led his parish in 1569 providing arms and horses for the defence of the realm.

In 1587 Edward succeeded his cousin as Lord Abergavenny and owner of estates in many counties. Newton passed successively after his death in 1589 to his son Edward (died 1622), to Edward's second son Christopher (died 1649), and to Christopher's grandson George (died 1665). In 1666 George's son, also George, presumably sold it to Joseph Langton, a Merchant Venturer of Bristol and in that year Mayor of the city. Like many a businessman before and since, Langton wanted to invest his profits in land and the social status that landed wealth alone could bring. His dignified marble memorial in the church at Newton ('worthy of Westminster Abbey', says Pevsner) bears witness, however, that possession is not always followed by succession. Joseph and his wife Frances buried five sons and three daughters, and only the marriage of one of the two surviving daughters to her cousin Robert Langton ensured that the name survived at Newton in the person of their son, another Joseph, to whom the mansion known as Newton Park must be due.

It seems to be universally agreed that the house was built in the years 1762-5. Pevsner, without hesitation, describes it as 'one of the finest country mansions of the 18th century in Somerset. Of the noble reticence characteristic of the School of Bath'. Its use first as a teacher training college and now as a college of higher education has not entirely destroyed the nobility, although the main front and curved wings are better seen without the inevitable collection of motor vehicles where once a carriage or two assembled for a drive in the park.

Pevsner did not know the name of the architect, but a reference made by J.C. Loudon in his book on the work of Humphrey Repton written in 1843 and a comparison with a similar house, Nuneham Park in Oxfordshire, make it seem likely that the designer was Stiff Leadbetter (died 1766).

The house is modest both in size and decoration; a main range of seven bays and two storeys with single-storeyed arcades curving gently forward to connect with service ranges of five bays. Each service bay has a large pediment and recessed cupola; the main house has a three-bay pediment with a semi-circular window, and the ground floor windows and central door have alternating pediments. The rest is without further decoration. The rear, garden front is plainer still, having only a single central canted bay with pedimented doorway. Inside, despite modern alterations for its present use, the original decorations are essentially preserved. Fine stucco ceilings and good fireplaces in well proportioned rooms surround a splendid central stair whose wrought iron balustrade climbs to a gallery and upper landing under a graceful glazed dome.

The setting of the house was all important. Mr Langton employed Lancelot Brown who, while turning the old castellated house into the picturesque ruin required by most of his patrons, produced from the Corston Brook which flowed in the valley to the north-west of the house two great lakes. Almost at the same time as this landscape was

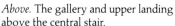

Above. The gallery and upper landing above the central stair.

Opposite top. The entrance front, of the 18th-century mansion.

Above right. Newton Park, an engraving of the house from across the lake created by 'Capability' Brown in the 18th century.

Left. A fine mansion in decay: painted decoration, 1949.

being thus improved, a stream from the same brook beyond the house was being diverted to serve some coal mines, decently screened, of course, from the gaze of those enjoying the park. The planting recommended by Brown still makes the approach as dramatic as he no doubt intended.

Joseph Langton, the builder of the mansion, had an only daughter Bridget, who in 1783 married young William Gore of Kiddington, Oxfordshire; not exactly a 'foreigner' since he was a grandson of Edward Gore of Barrow Gurney. In her right William assumed the additional name and arms of Langton and became active in the affairs of the county. He represented Somerset in Parliament three times between 1795 and 1832 but retained his Oxfordshire connection as colonel of that county's militia during the Napoleonic crisis. In his time Newton Park was evidently a centre of social and political power in the district.

William Gore Langton was succeeded on his death in 1847 by his grandson William Henry Powell Gore Langton, who preferred the house he had inherited through his mother's family, Hatch Park near Taunton. By one of those oddities of succession his son William Stephen by his wife Anna Grenville became in 1889 Earl Temple of Stowe. He died in 1902 and was followed by his eldest son Algernon (died 1940). Algernon's nephew sold the estate to the Duchy of Cornwall.

Newton Surmaville

Thomas Gerard described Mr Harbin's 'handsome new house' in 1633 as 'over the river', for at Trent, although then in Somerset, he was on the other side of the Yeo. The house is on a level terrace just above the meadows where the river divides Dorset from Somerset; and many of its owners have had Dorset rather than Somerset connexions. Indeed, the house has Dorset architectural parallels rather than any in Somerset.

Hidden from the road running along the hillside above by the trees of Newton Copse, the house and its accompanying farm are less than a mile from the noise of Yeovil; defended, as it were, by the borough boundary from the 20th century although now most recently part of the civil parish of Barwick.

The little manor of Newton has always been sheltered and secluded. Its origins date back to 1208, in the reign of King John, when 'Newenton' formed part of the dower of a Dorset heiress. On the death in 1221 of Emma Walensis the jury declared that Newton was held of the King in return for a rather peculiar service: that the owner should each Michaelmas give to the royal Exchequer a new table cloth measuring 10 ells in length and a towel measuring 5 ells. How long the owners of Newton actually rendered their table cloths and towels we shall never know; nor yet why Newton was so called, although the name implies a new settlement carved, presumably, from the great Domesday estate of Yeovil. The Surmaville addition is easier to explain, for Emma Walensis married as her first husband a member of the Dorset family called de Sarmunville, a name derived from their original home, a small village not far from Rouen.

The descent of the manor of Newton was many years ago traced with his usual care and accuracy by the Revd. Edward Bates Harbin, an heir of the original builders of the house. Joan de Surmaville who died in 1307 left, according to a formal inquest, a house and garden, some arable, pasture and wood, and a grove of alders. Her tenants, dwellers in the now-disappeared hamlet of Newton, numbered eight families. The Cricket family succeeded Surmavilles as owners of the manor and left behind from possible farming improvements made in the early 14th century the field named Cricketsham, land by the river made into valuable meadow. Less lasting was the chapel at Newton which Roger Langebroke and his wife had in the early 15th century when he was a tenant there.

Formal legal language described the estate in 1479 as 3 messuages,

11 tofts, a dovecot, a garden, and some 418 acres of land, much of it pasture. This estate Henry Burnell inherited in return for the ancient and curious duty, now converted by a cash-conscious Exchequer to an annual payment of 13s 4d. The formal language, however, does not hide a significant change. Those tofts sound very like the sites of earlier tenant farms, now given over to grass. Henry Burnell, owner of Newton and of much else at his death in 1490-1, left sheep and quantities of wool in legacies.

John Compton of Beckington, who bought Newton from Henry Burnell's son, came of a line of clothmen, and his son and grandson played the squire at Newton. But Joseph Compton found himself deeply in debt; he owed Sir Walter Raleigh £600. So he was obliged to sell, and the purchaser, one Robert Harbin of Wyke near Gillingham, yet another Dorset man to come to Somerset, duly became owner in 1608. Harbin presumably saw Newton less as a home for himself than as an investment for his family, for he was then an old man of 82, but an old man with vision. Within the next four years, if the date 1612 on the lead rainwater heads is proof enough, old Robert Harbin had built a new house on his new purchase, a house in which his descendants have lived ever since.

Robert Harbin's father probably came from Milton Abbas and he himself was by turn a Blandford mercer who rose to be a gentleman of Stalbridge and then of Gillingham. There can surely be no doubt of the breeding of the shrewd old man with the spectacles who sat for his portrait at the age of 93, still with two years of life to come. And to signify his pride in his new inheritance he applied for a grant of arms. Perhaps it was prophetic that it should have been that great antiquarian William Camden who as Clarencieux King of Arms gave Robert Harbin the right to bear the device which, formally described, reads: Azure a saltire voided between four spearheads erect or; and for a crest a cubit arm in armour holding a spur. Prophetic, because it was probably a descendant, the learned Dr George Harbin, a friend of Bishop Ken and a non-juror, who is still remembered for collecting and transcribing historical records including some relating to Somerset monasteries; and prophetic because to the present owner, Mrs Sophia Rawlins, and to her father, the Revd. Edward Bates Harbin, historians of Somerset are deeply indebted for their scholarship and hospitality.

The house Robert Harbin built is thought to have owed the style of its gabled north front to houses at Kingston Maurward and Wraxall, both in Dorset, and its chimneys to the now-demolished Stalbridge House in the same county. Its materials, however, were pure Somerset, the golden Ham stone which is the glory of so many buildings in the south of the county. Symmetry is the main characteristic of the three faces of the house. The north or entrance front, of two storeys with gabled attics, is divided by two two-storeyed square projections, the one providing windows on all three sides on both floors, the other the entrance porch below and a windowed bay

Robert Harbin, (1526-1621) aged 93, builder of the house.

The arms of Harbin, granted to Robert Harbin by William Camden, in a plaster overmantel.

The north front of the house built by Robert Harbin between 1608-1612.

John Harbin, (1565-1659) great-grandson of the builder, and a loyalist in the Civil War.

above. The arms over the porch commemorate a marriage of 1647 and might suggest an early modification to the original plan. The east or garden front is plainer, three shallow chimney breasts, the central one actually an entrance, perhaps the original main doorway. The chimneys are placed between four windows on each floor under a balustrade. The west front, slightly less regular, faces the hillside and is by far the simplest in detail, with two gables and a central porch. There are three windows on the ground floor and four above. The three fronts are all one room deep and range on three sides of a central courtyard, with kitchens in the west wing and other offices on the south side.

Structurally, the house was hardly altered for more than two centuries. The Harbins were evidently content with Robert's work and directed their energies elsewhere. A second Robert, grandson of the first, was for Parliament in politics, fighting in the skirmish called the battle of Babylon Hill not far from his home. He subsequently made his peace with the King as the moderates lost control of their cause; and for his innate loyalty was turned on by his erstwhile friends. He died in 1659 in debt and his heir, John, who had also suffered as a loyalist, was forced to sell some of the family estate.

John's heir at his death in 1672 was his younger son, William, whose marriage to Elizabeth Wyndham of Trent eventually brought to Newton not just some Wyndham portraits and fine pewter which are still there, but two caps and a knife which were relics from the time when the young Charles II, fleeing from the disaster at Worcester in 1651, was sheltered at Trent by Sir Francis Wyndham.

Throughout the 18th century Harbins made alliances with the modest gentry of the neighbourhood – the Swaynes of Tarrant

Gunville, the Gooddens of Nether Compton, the Abingtons of Sutton Bingham, the Wyndhams of Dinton and the Phelipses of Montacute. And three generations of eldest sons died without children. Yet one of these, George Harbin, made greater changes to the house than any of his family. Probably in the late 1840s he put a two-storeyed corridor into the courtyard behind the hall, making the bedrooms above more private, and changed the position of the stairs. Later in his life he added a large room at the end of the east wing, linked to conservatories beyond. The new room, lit by a fine window modelled on the great oriel in the Abbey Gatehouse at Montacute, has become the heart of the house for the two most recent owners of Newton.

The Revd. E.H. Bates, nephew and heir of Colonel Henry Harbin, inherited the house and estate in 1909 and took the additional name Harbin. For nine years until his untimely death he continued there his studies in the history of the house and county which he had begun many years before as a pioneer in local history, following the tradition of George Harbin, his distant relative. Historical enterprises such as the Somerset Record Society and Somerset and Dorset Notes and Queries found in him an active member, and it was entirely proper that he should have been the honorary local editor of the two early volumes of the Victoria History of Somerset, one of which appeared after his removal to Newton. His extensive library was then added to the volumes the house already contained in George Harbin's new room. Prebendary Bates Harbin's tradition of scholarship was inherited by his daughter Sophia, to whom many scholars owe a great deal for her kindly hospitality and deep learning.

A photograph taken in the 1930s of the east range with George Harbin's extension, lit by a copy of the Montacute Priory oriel.

George Harbin (1800-1886), who extended the east wing and filled part of the courtyard.

North Cadbury Court

It stands on its ridge looking across the broad valley to 'Camelot'. An avenue of limes conceals it from the village, and only from the churchyard can its west side be glimpsed. On the strength of a plain string course of stone a former owner dated that west side very precisely at 1417, possibly suspecting that the then lady of North Cadbury, planning to found a college of priests, might have thought to house them, even as a temporary measure, in part of her own dwelling.

That must be speculation, but it is likely that a house had long stood on the site, since Cadbury had been an important possession of the Newmarches and the Moels family in the 13th and early 14th centuries, long before Isabel, daughter and coheir of John, Lord Moels, married the Cornish William Botreaux. Their son William, first Lord Botreaux, served in military expeditions to Saxony and Portugal and was summoned to Parliament from 1368. His widow, a Daubeney of Barrington, outlived him by over 40 years, and had a grand design for Cadbury, for there she intended to found a college of priests. Papal approval was obtained in 1418 and the king granted his licence in 1422, but not until 1427 was the college formally established. By that time Dame Elizabeth had retired from Cadbury to the nunnery of Tarrant in Dorset. Her personal enthusiasm and drive were followed by success, but the church she rebuilt to be shared between the college and the parish was used by the parish alone and still stands, the windows in its chancel placed at such a height as to allow for the clergy stalls which were never built.

Elizabeth's great-granddaughter Margaret, in her own right Lady Botreaux, married Robert Hungerford, Lord Hungerford, and Cadbury may be said to have entered the centre of the political stage. Margaret's son and grandson were both executed for their Lancastrian sympathies, and her great-granddaughter Mary married into the hardly less fortunate Hastings family. This alliance, however, was perhaps of less significance to the house than to the part of the estate across the valley.

William, Lord Hastings, a loyal supporter of Edward IV, was evidently involved with the king's revival of the Order of the Garter at Windsor on the model of the Arthurian Round Table. His home at Ashby de la Zouch was near the home of Sir Thomas Malory. It is thus curious to find that one of Hastings' descendants should recount, perhaps as part of family lore, the tradition that the 'gallante

hil' above South Cadbury 'hathe bene a castel in times past called Camelot, wherin Sir Lancelot in King Arthur's time is fayned to have dwelled'. That is distinctly different from the report of John Leland, who wrote: 'The people can telle nothing ther but that they have herd say that Arture much resortid to Camalat'. Unless, of course, the people had been told the tale by a Hastings.

Cadbury had been but one of many manors owned by the Hungerfords, and was now in the hands of a family of even greater wealth. George Hastings, Mary Hungerford's son, was created Earl of Huntingdon in 1529 and in 1533 he also became Lord Botreaux, Lord Hungerford and Lord Moleyns. His son Francis, the second earl, was a close associate of the Duke of Northumberland at the end of Edward VI's reign but made peace with Queen Mary through his wife, a niece of Cardinal Pole. Francis died relatively young, but old enough to have fathered five sons and five daughters. The fifth son, Francis, was to play a significant part of the history of North Cadbury.

As the youngest son perhaps he could not have hoped for much, but when he came of age his eldest brother, the third earl, settled on him the manor of Market Bosworth; and in 1567 his marriage linked him with the family of the Earl of Rutland. He also had strong links with many who, like himself, were staunch advocates of the reformed religion. Yet for godly Sir Francis Hastings, his family, and especially his revered eldest brother, were of the greatest importance, and early in the 1580s he undertook the administration of his brother's estates to restore some order to the family finances.

In 1586 Lord Huntingdon granted his brother the four Somerset manors of North and South Cadbury, Holton and Maperton, thus giving him a base in his adopted county. Thus it was that he came to North Cadbury. What he found there by way of a house is not possible to say with accuracy, although the Revd James Bennett, brought up in the house, said that much of the surviving walling was medieval, and another writer has claimed that a lobby on the top floor showed a roof of what had been a great hall. This is perhaps the hall in the west range where the date 1581 was reported in the 1790s, a range which appears more likely to have been of the early 16th century.

Sir Francis evidently determined on an extensive rebuilding, which was under way by the autumn of 1589, when he was living in West Camel. In a letter dated December 1592 he told his brother that his house was 'in good forwardnes' and he seems to have moved in during the course of 1593. That house, with its remarkable glass, is the core of the present building. Lost paintings of Sir Francis's house, depict a symmetrical hall range with two broad wings behind; its facade is balanced by a porch and a bay window. Porch and square bay still remain, but while the windows on each side of them retain the symmetry of the ground and first floors, the second floor appears irregular since four gables have had to be arranged over six bays.

Left. Some of the late-medieval roof timbers in the west range, a survival from the Hungerford house.

Opposite top. The 18th-century south range, probably the work of Francis Mompesson (died 1796).

Opposite below. The church of North Cadbury, rebuilt as a collegiate church by 1427.

The windows are a remarkable feature of the north front, all mullioned and transomed. Those in the bay and at each end of the range on the first floor have eight lights and double transoms.

What still survives of Hastings' original work inside is a fine ribbed plaster ceiling on the first floor, decorated with foliage and ogee shapes. More remarkable are the panels of stained glass, originally twenty-four in number, perhaps designed to illustrate Hastings' political connexions; for they display the arms of the great and the good of Tudor England. Was this a piece of family propaganda? Such examples of family piety are usually done with at least one eye on benefits for the heir, but Sir Francis and his wife were childless, and North Cadbury was soon to pass outside the family which, despite changes of name, had owned it for so long. In 1596 Sir Francis Hastings lost both his beloved elder brother and his wife; and he soon afterwards sold North Cadbury, the manor and the newly-created house, to his friend Matthew Ewens, a Baron of the Exchequer.

The descent of the property from the Ewens family to the Newmans, and from the Newmans to the Bennetts has not yet been satisfactorily told, but it is certain that Richard Newman was in possession by 1684. The arms of Mompesson on a doorway in the grounds record the marriage of Francis Hollis Newman to Eleanor Mompesson. Their sons Francis and Charles (died 1734) perhaps held it in turn and were followed by Charles's son Francis (died 1796). The last evidently sold the house and estate to James Bennett of London, who by 1799 had so established himself in Somerset that he became sheriff. To Bennett, probably, is owed the radical alteration on the

south side of the house where the courtyard was converted into a room on each floor, that on the ground floor with a large bow window. The older windows on the south front were sashed, giving the whole front a generally classical style.

A house which has grown in distinct stages is not necessarily ideal for modern living. Mr (later Sir) Archibald Langman, C.M.G., entertained members of the Somerset Archaeological Society there in 1913 when the house was undergoing extensive restoration. The interior was re-arranged and much renewed, involving the use of disguised steel columns. Some earlier owner had removed a gatehouse and square forecourt through which the house had been approached from the north. The Bennetts certainly left their mark with their crest over the main door and also with a bath, complete with hot and cold water supply, in the west wing. The Langman contribution, typical of someone concerned for preserving village community life, was to allow the village club the use of two rooms in the older part of the house. Sir Archibald died in 1949.

The contribution of the present owner in maintaining the house in modern conditions is almost as laudable as that of the builders. Mrs Montogomery is, indeed, truly the successor of Sir Francis Hastings – not only in her care for the house but in concern for the land. Like Hastings she, too, owns Camelot. It was with her support that the great hill fort was made to yield its riches in the excavations carried out there between 1966 and 1970; with her cooperation visitors can walk on those ramparts and imagine themselves back in Dark Age Britain or under the spell of High Romance. The view of the Georgian face of the house on the ridge across the valley may not beckon, but those who seek the church beside it will be richly rewarded and will catch a tantalizing glimpse of the Court beyond the churchyard wall.

Orchard Wyndham

There is a reticence about Orchard Wyndham, a modesty. The decorated Victorian barge boards suggest something almost suburban, but paintings of the 18th century depict a mansion of impressive proportions from which whole wings have been removed. Its site, in a bowl of woodland and pasture at the northern end of the Brendon hills, is very much part of the reticence; the modesty is typical of the family which has lived here since the 16th century.

M.R. James, the often irascible Provost of Eton and author of famous ghost stories, stayed here for two days in 1932 visiting 'stout and bearded William [Wyndham]' who had given an organ to Eton College, one of his many generous benefactions. 'An ancient house', wrote James, 'smoking room kept locked (but unlocked for me, and smoking permitted in the Library)'. Others appreciated – and continue to benefit from – the benefactions of William Wyndham in the fields of public education more generously. William himself, typically modest, recorded of one of his own forebears, George, 3rd Earl of Egremont, of Orchard and Petworth, that in the last six years of his life (he died in 1837) his charities were said to have amounted to £1,200,000. William's own contribution was a more modest £40,000.

The only immodesty, if such it be, is to name the house after the

The west front, with the Victorian barge boards beneath the eaves.

Part of the roof of the early 16th-century Hall.

owner; but that is surely justified and probably not of their own doing. Yet the Wyndhams were not the creators of the estate which bears their name. Thomas Palmer, writing in the early 18th century, found at Orchard a charter of Thomas Orchard dated 1287 which suggested a house already standing here and an estate in the making, but he had to confess himself unable to explain the building which stood in his own time: 'all the rest was built at different times, and some parts seem so ancient as it may be believed they were built by the primitive owners of the name of Orchard'.

The Orchard family name came to end when an heiress, Joan, married Richard Popham of Alfoxton. Their daughter, also Joan, married in 1448 John Sydenham of Combe (died 1464), the first of four Johns to occupy the estate. John Leland, Henry VIII's Antiquary, credited their son, another John, with 'moste part or almost all the good building of Orcharde'. He died in 1521. Until very recently only one part of the house could be accurately dated to this John's time, and that part has now gone. It was a chapel for which he received a licence in 1499. But restoration work on the roof, as so often in an old house, has revealed much about its past.

The present house comprises buildings ranged around two court-yards, of which those around the southern courtyard are the oldest. A small window buried in the range on its northern side and now in the very centre of the house, leads Dr Katherine Wyndham, herself a trained historian, to believe that there lay a hall perhaps built by Thomas Orchard himself, with a slightly later solar to the west. That hall is now roofed by four arch-braced raised crucks, constructed in the 15th century and smoke blackened. Running north from the east end of the hall is a range (now the present service range) of about 1500, with an arch-braced collar beam roof; and from the solar per-haps ran the original kitchen. That, too, is roofed with raised crucks which have been blackened through smoke. The courtyard is com-pleted at its southern side by another range, probably of the 15th century, including a corbelled chimney.

Where John Sydenham's chapel stood is a matter for speculation, but it is possible that it formed a wing built forward from the hall. Within twenty years or so the house was again increased in size, for a new hall was built, perhaps with the chapel forming two sides of a second, northern courtyard, the hall having a cross-wing with a par-lour (later the Library) and a solar. The hall has an open arch-braced collar-beam roof of eight bays and became the main axis of the house, the place of passage and hospitality.

Now enter the Wyndhams. John Sydenham died young and with-out children in 1526, leaving his property to be divided between his two sisters, Jane and Elizabeth. Both ladies were clearly prizes for any young man. Elizabeth, possibly the younger, was soon married to John Wyndham, a member of a respectable Norfolk family; the other was married somewhat later to Sir Thomas Brydges. Each couple then held strictly half the inheritance: one half of the house called Orchard Place, one half of all the buildings, one half of two adjoining gardens called Hyll garden and Knott garden, half an orchard and half of all the demesne lands at a distance. Of course, while strictly legal, the division was probably not practical, so in May 1530 the two couples agreed on a deal. Brydges sold his share to Wyndham for 100 marks (£66.66p).

John Wyndham had already had an interesting career, spending his early years in the French Court, according to family tradition, in the retinue of Princess Mary when she married King Louis XII. Perhaps after his marriage he continued as a courtier and he was knighted at Edward VI's coronation in 1547 'for royal service done'. But if this perhaps marked the end of his Court life, he then settled down to enlarge his house, apparently adding a third courtyard to the north, where the front was rebuilt about 1500, and a fourth to the west. John furnished the house, if his will is a guide, with considerable luxury including hangings, carpets, cushions, elaborate household equipment and personal possessions.

Sir John Wyndham, 1560.

The linenfold panelling of his time, once in the house, was given to Wadham College, Oxford.

Sir John died in 1574, outliving both his wife and his son and heir. His successor was his grandson, another John, who had received under his father's will a 'tablet' of gold, a gold chain, 29 pairs of gold 'agletts', a nest of silver bowls with a cover, a silver gilt salt and a silver cup parcel gilt. The Wyndhams may not have been ostentatious but they were adequately wealthy. When in 1581 young John Wyndham came of age his estate was not, however, large and was scattered around the parish of St Decuman in Watchet, Washford, and Williton. His house and demesne was, in that technical feudal sense, not his own: it was held of Sir Edward Stradling as of the manor of Halsway, a link going back time out of mind.

The young heir, also heir to the family estate in Norfolk and of his mother's Wadham properties, was more affluent than his grandfather, but no particular part of the house can be ascribed to him. Thomas Gerard, writing in 1633, seems to suggest that his energies were expended rather on himself than on public service, which his rank and wealth might have indicated. In contrast his son Sir William — and his memorial inscription is surely to be believed — 'devoted himself and his very weighty interest' not only to the interest of the Crown but in healing wounds left in the social and political fabric left by the Civil War.

Orchard Wyndham itself had not been untouched in the conflict. Sir John was too old to play an active part: he was well over eighty when war broke out and he died in 1645. His cousins Edmund and Francis were prominent for the King, his son John married the sister of Sir Ralph Hopton, a prominent Royalist commander, though he himself may have sympathised with the other side. Perhaps this was the reason why Francis Wyndham, the commander of Dunster, in June 1644 led a foray to Orchard which relieved Sir John of £4,000 worth of plunder, something like a fifth of his personal goods. Sir John's heir, also John, did not survive for long and from 1649 Orchard, like many country estates, escaped the burden of sequestration. William, heir to his grandfather Sir John, unlike his more partisan cousins of Trent and Kentsford, was evidently for peace and compromise; he was prepared to accept a baronetcy from Cromwell and sat for Taunton in Richard Cromwell's parliament in 1659. But, Royalist at heart, his title was restored by Charles II and he served in parliament until 1680, although more at home hunting in the country and proposing improvements in the trade of Somerset's ports. The rich wainscoting of the Hall and Library at Orchard are his surviving contribution to the house.

Sir William died in 1683. The family records for the time of his son Edward (died 1695) suggest a little excitement in 1685 during Monmouth's Rebellion when the parish of St Decuman sent six men to fight for the King and another to carry arms to Taunton. Perhaps

The monument to Sir William Wyndham (died 1683) in St. Decuman's church.

those arms included the twenty six muskets 'taken away and lost' from the collection of sixty held in the Hall.

Edward's son William succeeded in 1695 at the age of ten. He became a man of wide cultural interests, and entered politics in 1710 as a Tory. In 1712 he became Secretary at War, in 1713 Chancellor of the Exchequer, and in 1714 the chief Treasury Commissioner. But the arrival of the Hanoverians suddenly brought to an end his brilliant career. He remained a Member of Parliament until his death in 1740, leading the opposition to Walpole. An early and rash attempt to lead a rising in favour of the Stuarts led to imprisonment in the Tower, but he was never tried. Orchard Wyndham became the centre of political opposition and Sir William the mouthpiece of his friend and mentor, Henry, Viscount Bolingbroke.

There were more than sixty rooms at Orchard at the end of the 17th century, of which at least twenty-three were service rooms. An inventory of 1697 recorded over forty beds. In his long period of ownership Sir William created features still recognised today: the large front door and fanlight above at the centre of the north range is his work, and inside the Hall the rusticated stone fireplace. More significant is the disappearance of the northern courtyard, which was roofed over and into which a grand staircase gave access to the rooms above. Sir William also rebuilt the rooms on the west side of the former courtyard, including the present Drawing Room.

The landscape painting by Robert Griffier which hangs in the Hall should not be taken as an accurate view by any stretch of the imagination — not accurate for the landscape features, the geography or the architecture. But in the massive sprawling house in the picture is Griffier's way of showing the north, west and east sides of the house in the same plane. Its immediate surroundings may be more accurate: a tree-lined avenue stretching up the hill to what must be Black Down, and the village of Stream across the deer park with faint traces nearer the house of what might be either a circular pond or an island or a mound. Black Down was replanted by Sir William 1707, after destruction in the Great Storm of 1703, around a tower which can be glimpsed in Griffier's painting. His contributions to the grounds over more than twenty years may be gauged by the agreement his heir Sir Charles Wyndham made with John Headford of Williton: Headford would live in the garden house rent free, run the kitchen garden, clear the walks, clip hedges and trees and repair the vistas in Black Down wood beyond the park. He would keep the bowling green ready for use, tend the fruit trees in the garden west of the house, keep the courts on the north side and the walks along the Williton drive. Headford could sell all the produce of the kitchen garden and the walnuts from the park so long as the family table was first supplied; and he was to preserve all seeds for the coming year, find his own poles for vines, espaliers, peas and french beans.

Sir William Wyndham's first wife was a daughter of the Duke of Somerset and in 1750 Sir Charles found himself on the death of his

Opposite top. The painting of Orchard Wyndham by Robert Griffier (c.1688–c.1760).

Opposite below. The north front, showing scars of earlier buildings and George Frederick Wyndham's Gothick window over the main door.

uncle the owner of vast estates in six counties, a principal residence at Petworth in Sussex and the title of Earl of Egremont. Orchard, surplus to immediate requirements, was partially let: the dairy house, laundry range, the old garden house once occupied by the chaplain and the cook, and the stables became the centre of a farm whose land included the old garden, the park, and the bowling green.

The house was not, of course, neglected. An account book of repairs there in 1764-5 still belongs among the Petworth archives, and so does an inventory of its furniture made in 1773. But it seems likely that George Wyndham, the third earl, demolished the Tudor wings to north and west at some date before 1816, bringing the house to more manageable proportions. George Francis Wyndham, nephew of George and fourth earl, succeeded in 1837 and began spending money at Orchard: rooms at the north-east corner, the Gothick window over the main door, the conservatory, a fine chimneypiece in the Drawing Room, the arch linking the north-east wing to the new gazebo tower built over the ice house. His time at Orchard was short, for he died in 1845, but his widow lived there for another thirty years. After her death in 1877 a sale of contents took place at the Egremont Hotel in Williton and another of livestock at the Williton Monthly Auction. The curious collection of effects included a stereoscope, an invalid chair, drawing instruments, a shower bath, two flutes, two swords, three croquet sets, two tennis sets, carriages, phaetons, a landau and a charabanc. Among the livestock were her Ladyship's three 'well known' grey carriage horses. The total estate amounted in Somerset alone to 8,365 acres.

The fourth Earl of Egremont left no direct heirs, but on his widow's death Orchard passed to William Wyndham, a country landowner from Dinton in Wiltshire. His son, also William, made Orchard his only home after his father's death, and it was to this shy man that education and archaeology in Somerset and Wiltshire owe so much. His death in 1950 had, sadly, to be followed by the sale of much property which had belonged to the family for generations, but his heir, his nephew George, abandoned a diplomatic career and took up the challenge. For more than thirty years until his premature death in 1982 he accepted wide responsibilities in public service on bench and in council, the first member of the family to have been sheriff of Somerset since Sir William in 1679. Since his death the restoration of the house has been in the care of his daughter Katherine, whose historical insight and deep sense of family tradition make her the entirely fitting guardian of a house with such a long family ancestry.

A detail of the plasterwork frieze on the first floor.

Poundisford Park

The outline of the 16th-century carrack cut into wet plaster and discovered on the wall of the 'Queen's Room'.

Medieval floor tiles, perhaps from Taunton Priory, in an upstairs passage.

The almost ghostly form of a carrack lightly cut into wet plaster when the 'Queen's Room' was first created, the medieval tiles in the passage between the top of the spiral stairs from the Hall and the former muniment room, the many fragments of carved stone used as rubble in the walls, and the quatrefoil frieze on the outside of the Hall chimney of Poundisford Park illustrate very aptly the origin of the house. Family tradition that its builder about 1546 was William Hill, who had 'employed himself as a merchant in foreign parts', explains the carrack remarkably well, and family tradition is confirmed by State Papers which describe Hill as owner of a 50-ton ship at Minehead in 1543. His business connections were evidently not just with Minehead, for he was trading in wine and iron through Bridgwater about 1550 and he married two of his sons to the daughters of John Hassard of Lyme, of a family which traded there and at Bridport. Hill himself married a Dorset woman as his second wife.

So much for Hill's resources, but there is more than a suggestion that, as a careful businessman, he built with an eye on cost. That family tradition, possibly waxing rather lyrical, tells that he went on a long voyage to the Guinea Coast of Africa and that on his return he discovered his father dead and his elder brother become a gentleman, possessor of part of the Bishop of Winchester's deer park at Pitminster, where he was busy building himself a country house (now Poundisford Lodge). The story goes on that William set about emulating his brother with some alacrity by acquiring the lease of the other half of the park and by building there 'as good a house or better as quickly'. The Vivian-Neals had reason to believe the truth of this: restoration in 1929 and during the past few years revealed much re-used stone and some evidence of poor construction. The stonework, and the tiles in the passage, may well have come from the buildings of Taunton's former Augustinian priory, dissolved in 1539.

But when did William build? There are no convenient dates to be found in the building, and the initials E.R. with the Royal Arms on the west wall of the Hall could as well stand for Elizabeth as for Edward VI. Writers in the 1930s saw distinct shades of Barrington both in layout and detail, and therefore thought the date 1546 was reasonable. Now that Barrington has been dated to about 1570 the earlier date begins to look more than a little shaky. Yet there is something still rather medieval about Poundisford: buttresses, four-centred arches in the Hall, arched lights in the windows are late-Perpendicular. Its layout harks back too: a central hall with large chimney stack beside a spiral stair; matching alcoves for the oriels where the dais would have been, but which actually lead to a conventional west cross-wing where parlours and garderobe, were later to be divided between Library (former Justice Room), sitting-room and staircase. The screen has large circular muntins probably dating from the 1550s. The screens passage runs along the east end of the Hall, and across it is a matching service wing and a matching garderobe, the wing later to be divided between Dining-room, staircase and kitchen. The merchant seems to have been conservative in his tastes.

In twenty years the merchant became a gentleman. Is there, perhaps, a connection between his second marriage into a minor Dorset gentry family and the grant in 1570 of a coat of arms? And might not his marriage and acquired gentility be the excuse for the transformation of his house not by any expensive building programme but by the insertion of fine plaster ceilings. The best is in the Hall where thin ribs form star patterns and where fashionable pendants droop down over the interior, notably around the curiously coved edges. The corner pendants declare their creators with the initials W.H. and L.H. for William and Lucy Hill. At the same time the gallery above the screen was transformed into a passage by a partition pierced only by a little bay window, permitting a delightful view into the Hall.

More plasterwork is to be found in the Hall Chamber, the King's and the Queen's rooms (the Hill crest in the later must be of 1570 or later) and the Gallery, where the thin ribs form squares or stars. There are also robust Renaissance friezes in Hall and Gallery. Similarities with work at Mapperton, Dorset, are not, given Hill's Dorset connections, very surprising.

William Hill evidently lived to a great age, for the successful merchant of 1543 survived until 1594. In his will, drawn up less than two years earlier, he mentioned three sons and three daughters. Roger, his heir and named after his merchant grandfather, died in 1609 leaving an annuity and a suite of rooms for his widow. He seems to have left no obvious work in the house. Neither, indeed, did his son William (died 1642) nor his grandson Roger, although the latter's political views made him an acceptable replacement for a Royalist M.P. for Bridport in 1645, and some kind of good fortune prevented him from being a judge of his king and hence the subject of Restoration malice. He died, as he had probably lived, with a greater interest among the legal community of the capital than in his paternal inheritance. He was buried in 1667 in the Temple Church. But Chief Baron Hill, named after his Cromwellian appointment in the Exchequer, left important notes on his family's history, perhaps to replace the muniments which the Royalists may well have stolen when they rifled the house during the siege of Taunton.

Opposite top. The north front of the 16th-century house with the late 17th-century dining room wing and later offices.

Opposite bottom. The south front, the centre festooned with leaden gutters and downpipes and a medieval quatrefoil frieze.

Opposite top. The Gallery. The window fastenings and glass are of the same date as the ribbed plaster ceiling, c. 1570.

Opposite bottom. The Dining Room, originally built in 1692 but given its present appearance in about 1738.

Roger's son William's initials and those of his wife Hester greet the visitor by the entrance door on the magnificent leaden tank there which also bears the date 1671 and which once caught rainwater from the elaborate gutters which festoon the south side of the house. The contemporary rainwater heads bear the arms of Hill impaling Muschamp. This William Hill died in 1680 and was followed by his lawyer half-brother, Sir Roger. Either William or Sir Roger made a significant addition to the house, the Parlour (later Library) ceiling. It bears an oval central motif with the Hill crest of a dove at the centre and around it bands of scrolls and a wreath. There are foliage panels in each corner. The pattern for the work may well have been the ceiling at Forde Abbey, not far away and usually ascribed to about 1650. This, and similar work at Gaulden, may be ten or twenty years later and by an inferior hand.

Sir Roger's interests moved away from Somerset and Poundisford if, indeed, they had ever been here, for he was London born and married a wife from East Anglia. During his ownership, and perhaps about 1690, the original symmetry of the house was destroyed by the addition of a wing at the north-east corner to form a dining-room. Sir Roger himself settled at Denham in Buckinghamshire, but Poundisford remained in the family until 1706 when he sold it to Dr Simon Welman, a London physician with Taunton and other Somerset connections. This was the beginning of Welman ownership of both Poundisford Park and the neighbouring Poundisford Lodge which lasted until 1869.

The Welmans in the person of Isaac (died 1782) apparently created the charming ante-chamber to the Dining-room by constructing the screen of Ionic pillars and adding the cornice and fireplace about 1738. But perhaps because the family had other, and Evangelical, interests their alterations at the Park were modest. A Servants' Hall and other domestic offices were added at the south-east about 1825, but the house excaped other destructive modernization. Owned by the Helyar family of Poundisford Lodge from 1869, the Park was let to a succession of tenants until 1928 when it was bought by Arthur Vivian-Neal.

Under Anthony Methuen the house was carefully restored and its history traced (so far as was possible) by its new owner, whose contribution to the history of Somerset as Chairman of the County Records Committee was immense. As sheriff of the county, he stood in that long line of public servants and in particular in succession to a former owner of Poundisford, Isaac Welman (sheriff in 1709-10).

Poundisford's site was created long before the house, for it was the southern part of the deer park of the bishops of Winchester, lords of the great manor of Taunton Deane since Saxon times. The park had been created by the thirteenth century and may have been the one re-stocked by order of King John in 1210-11. The garden seems perfect for the house, simple and informal, merging on the north over a ha-ha into the ancient park pasture. There is the nice, contrasting

Above. The house from the north west.

Left. The brick gazebo of c.1700 at the western end of the garden.

formality of the pretty brick gazebo of about 1700 at the western end of the garden.

Part of the house has been open to visitors during the summer, but throughout the year people find their way to the former, safely detached, original Kitchen, to the east of the house beside the Pump Court. There the Wellhouse Restaurant has been established for several years, offering a taste of that modestly gracious living for which succeeding families at Poundisford have been famous for four centuries.

Stavordale Priory

Early in June 1443 John Bloxwych, a Carmelite friar and bishop of the unlikely see of Holar in Iceland, was commissioned by Bishop John Stafford of Bath and Wells to dedicate, consecrate and bless the nave, choir and chancel of the conventual church of Stavordale, hidden away in the wooded hills in the north of Charlton Musgrove parish and close to the Wiltshire border. To rebuild their church in its entirety would have been far beyond the slender means of the little community of Augustinian canons who had been established there since the beginning of the 13th century, but they had always been fortunate in their patrons and benefactors. Probably the house had been founded by a Lovel of Castle Cary; Nicholas Seymour, successor to the Lovels, was described as patron in the mid 14th century and his brother Richard was buried in 1400 'in the new chapel of the priory' as befitted founders' kin. Already by that time the Stourtons, who themselves also claimed descent from the Lovels, had surpassed them in power and prestige. Taking their name from the parish just over the Wiltshire border to the east, they had made themselves sufficiently important by 1374 to found a chantry at Stavordale at the altar of St James, the patron in whose name the house was dedicated. The altar stood under the bell tower. There, thanks to an endowment given by John Stourton, mass was to be said for the soul of himself, his wife and their parents. A corpse excavated on the site of the tower in 1981 may well be that of John himself.

John's son, also John, of Preston Plucknett, whose daughter was to be mistress of Brympton, clearly saw Stavordale as his spiritual home and made of it his family's mausoleum. In his will drawn up in November 1438 he assumed (surely quite correctly) that he would be buried there and requested that his body should be taken to his burial on his best waggon, drawn by his best oxen. Waggon and oxen were then to remain after the funeral for a 'memorial' of his soul. But, after detailing what his widow was to receive, and making particular family bequests, he revealed what had become his greatest concern, the rebuilding of the church of the priory:

'I will that the church of Stavordale and the cloister there shall be completed in all things, as well in glazing the windows as in other buildings there to be done, and that the expenses and costs thereof shall be borne by my executors ... I will that the aforesaid church shall be throughout honestly paved with tile of my arms and the arms of my mother ...'.

The monastic seal over the entrance to Stavordale Priory.

Above. The former Priory church from the south-west, showing the arch leading from the nave to the former tower.

Right. The east window, stone panelling and vaulting in Lord Zouche's Chapel of Jesus, c.1526.

And for himself and his wife he directed burial between the stalls in the choir, providing already 'images' of each to be placed on the tomb which, when completed, was to be enclosed with iron bars and was to have a lectern at the head. Such a tomb was only suitable for a second founder, and it was the church, choir and chancel which John Stourton's generosity had made possible that the bishop of Holar consecrated in 1443, four years after the donor's death.

So the canons, eight in number in 1400, six in 1533, continued on their quiet, undistinguished way. And another will reveals the next — and last — stage in the building of the priory church. In it John, Lord Zouche and Seynt Maur, successor to the Lovels of Castle Cary, requested burial in the chapel of Jesus 'by me newe buylded in the Priory of Staverdell' where he had already endowed a chantry staffed by two priests who were to celebrate mass on Wednesdays and Fridays. In addition, every year on the day of his death the prior and convent were to sing dirges 'while the worlde shall endure'. Zouche was evidently a careful man, and left detailed instructions to ensure that his dispositions were carried out, providing worthy trustees to secure a proper income from his estate. There had, it seems, been some family trouble between Lord Zouche and his son, and the former had retired to the priory, where he occupied a 'lodging' somewhere in the precinct. Under the will Sir John FitzJames was given this house 'provided always that in any wise [he] shall not suffer my sonne Sir John Zouche to occupie nie abide in the same'.

John, Lord Zouche, died in 1526 and his son and namesake did not follow him as he had expected; the FitzJameses retained possession until 1544 when Stavordale passed to Richard Zouche. But after all his careful plans, Lord Zouche would, perhaps, have been alarmed when in 1533, in face of increasing financial problems, the canons were absorbed into the larger Augustinian community of Taunton priory. At least the house in consequence survived the dissolution of the smaller monasteries in 1536, but when Taunton fell in 1539, the two remaining canons at Stavordale yielded too. The two chantry priests continued, however, for they were independent of the monastic endowment. Indeed, the chapel had probably even by that date become in effect part of the house occupied by 1539 by Richard Zouche, who wrote in that year to Thomas Cromwell to secure possession. In 1548 the chapel was said to have been 'scituate within the saide Lorde Zouche's house'. The church of the canons had, it seems, already become a dwelling.

Richard Zouche stayed at Stavordale until 1571 when Nicholas Wylkynson acquired the property. Two centuries and more later, in 1782, Moulton Messiter sold it to Edward Burford. The latter, probably the 'Dr Burford, of Banbury in the county of Oxford', mentioned as owner in 1791, were both absentee owners; the remains of the priory had come to be a farmhouse and barns. Yet that relatively humble status and remote site ensured that what John Stourton had rebuilt and the Zouches had lodged in survived in a remarkable way.

Opposite top. South-east view of the former chancel, with the chapel and modern range on north side.

Opposite bottom. The Priory church from the north across the garden.

The chancel roof and the outline of the great east window, in what is now an upstairs bedroom.

At the end of the 18th century the church was a barn, but 'two good Gothick arches', carved roof timbers, a bell turret with a bell, a stoup and shields with the arms of Zouche and Lovel bore witness to its past. In the house, upstairs rooms had carved intersecting roof beams and stone vaulting. So it remained until the early years of the 20th century.

About 1902 a gentleman recognised the possibilities of farmhouse and barn. Frederick Sage brought in the distinguished architect F.E. Colcutt, then President of the Royal Institute of British Architects, to create for him a country house. Colcutt's touch was light but sure. The priory church, still with traces of its 13th-century origins but without its bell tower, was carefully restored, although 18th-century windows in the former choir were retained and effectively incorporated into the design. The building was not, of course, large enough for Mr Sage's requirements, and Colcutt added a north wing which time and the present owner's magnificent garden have blended so splendidly into a harmonious whole.

Ston Easton Park

The Hippisleys or Ipslays were many and varied. Nicholas and Edward, 'off ther sensuall and uncharitable mynde', were two of the miscreants who in 1533 demolished the dam which penned in the waters of Emborough Pool, thereby destroying the fish of which the Carthusians of Hinton were the owners. William Hypsley of nearby Midsomer Norton, owner of land in Emborough, Farrington, Stratton and Chilcompton, all in the rolling sheep country of Mendip, died in the winter of 1524 leaving to his son John a sheep farm called Tunnerys or Turners Court. It was probably that John who with his wife Agnes leased the farm of Ston Easton from the Augustinian canons of Bruton for a rent of £13 10s a year, a lease renewed in favour of John and his sons John and William in 1537. And when, two years later, the unthinkable happened and the house at Bruton was dissolved, the Hippisleys remained as the Crown's sitting tenants, prosperous enough by 1544 to find the sum of £557 3s 4d to become outright owners.

John Hippisley died in 1558 and John followed John for five generations, all four successors students of the law. John (1530-70), son of the purchaser, was 'the most successful country practitioner of his time', and served as Recorder of Bristol, a Justice of the Peace and M.P. for Wells 1562-7. He lived mostly at Cameley which he bought in 1561. His son John (1554-1608) married a daughter of the Horners of Mells and lived at Emborough and then at Cameley until his grandmother's death in 1586 when he at last moved into the manor house at Ston Easton, which she had occupied ever since the first John's death nearly thirty years before.

The next John Hippisley (1604-64), with Robert Harbin of Newton Surmaville and a few others, 'gave the parliamentarian leadership a respectable appearance' at the beginning of the Civil War, following the lead of his father-in-law John Preston of Cricket St Thomas. He, too, was living at Emborough at least when he made his will. His mother had lived at Ston Easton until her death in 1638-9.

Sir Nikolaus Pevsner, faced like every other visitor with the massive Classical facade of the house as he came down the drive, concentrated his attention on the 18th-century work in the building, mentioning almost as an afterthought that 'the west wing is older than the rest of the house'. Two blocked mullioned windows and some 'Queen Anne' panelling may have been all the visible evidence (except the extra floors at that end of the house) when he went there

in the 1950s. After essential structural work had been begun by the present owners from 1978 that older house began to be revealed. It was, apparently, a tall gabled house of five bays and parts were, remarkably, of five storeys, including cellars and attics. Its date, however, presents some difficulties, for the roof is the only clue to its form and age. Tom Foster, the architect for the restoration work, thought that its earliest part was Tudor with wings added in the 17th century.

A map belonging to the Hippisley family and now in the County Record Office offers a solution. Its exact date is not known, but it was drawn for Preston Hippisley, son of the Parliamentarian John, who was in possession between 1672 and his death in 1723. It portrays the houses in Ston Easton village, each drawn with remarkable detail. There, east of the parish church, where Manor Farm now stands, was the manor house, some distance from the village centre; and in the heart of the settlement on what may once have been a very large green and is now part of the grounds of the house, stood Preston Hippisley's tall and impressive house of five bays with a central tall gabled porch, the very house still to be found in the heart of the present mansion. And north of the house was a large fishpond, while to the east stood the house of Thomas Dory.

The Palladian south front with its flanking pavilions.

Mr Hippisley's New House, c.1700, from a family estate map, showing the original village later removed to create the park.

Who actually built Preston Hippisley's house the map does not reveal, but it is there described as 'new'. That word, of course, may have been in use for years, and was new only in the sense that it had evidently replaced the old manor house by the church. In the form in which it appears on the map it is, on balance, likely to have been the work of Preston Hippisley himself.

The great transformation from relatively modest house to Palladian mansion was, it is generally agreed, the work of John Hippisley Coxe, grandson of Preston Hippisley and son of Margaret, the last of her line of Hippisleys, by John Coxe of Wiltshire. Someone drew up a grand design which has also survived among the Hippisley archives. It bears no name and no date but it reveals the outline of an apparently new house surrounded by a splendid garden design. The new house, shown only on plan, had a central bay slightly recessed with a wing half as deep as the main house protruding to the west. It is shown standing above a lake, clearly enough the fishpond of the earlier map transformed to fit the spirit of the new plan with cascades and robing house at one end, and at the other a dam concealed as a grotto and more cascades. To the south of the house was a formal parterre, overlooked on one side by an 'esplanade' of grass in front of a 'saloon' or garden house with an arched centre. An avenue stretched south with woods each side, some curving, some in formal designs. To the south-east was a kitchen garden with fruit trees and hothouses.

There was in this design a serious problem: in the valley beside the dam and overlooking the grotto was the home of Mrs Dory, perhaps the widow of Thomas Dory who had lived there in Preston Hippisley's time. The problem was to provide Mrs Dory with access to her house and at the same time to disguise the fact that she lived so close. A road was planned which would be hidden when the woods had grown, and would run past village cottages and under a bridge linking the kitchen garden with the house. And so that her house should not be seen from the formal garden, a stable block and farm buildings, no doubt entirely picturesque, were placed facing the garden house across the parterre.

The plan was never fully carried out. Perhaps Mrs Dory died; certainly by the time John Hippisley Coxe succeeded, the fashion for that kind of formality had passed, although the grand prospect to the south across a wide expanse of park was undertaken. To achieve that a road was diverted, part of the village removed. Mogg, one of the cottagers whose hovel interrupted the prospect, had to be bought out. Only the village church survived for that was, by definition, romantic. How ironic that two centuries after all this creativity, there should have been a serious proposal to demolish the mansion and later, when it was being restored by a descendant of the Moggs, that the park should have been threatened with a by-pass.

John moved to the house on the death of his mother in 1738 and remained there until his death in 1769. His appointment as a Freeman

Ston Easton Park, a romantic view published in 1791.

of nearby Bath soon after coming into possession was a recognition of his social status and perhaps of his tastes. A family memorial in Ston Easton church spoke of 'his inclination, early fixed to a country residence . . . [which] . . . caused him often to refuse a public station in Parliament'. His marriage to the Devon heiress Mary Northleigh, a lady 'born in the affluence of fortune', is thought to have provided the means and their coat of arms is placed above the front entrance. Yet the attribution is not unanimously agreed: a strong local tradition argues that the work was perhaps begun by John and finished by his son Richard (1742-86). That young man, according to the family memorial, 'matured by all the advantages of refined education and foreign travel', three times took the county seat in Parliament in the Whig interest which his father had refused, and played the prosperous squire in the social and commercial circles of Bristol.

Details of the decoration inside the house actually have more in common with Bristol than with Bath, although the plain and severe exterior, relieved only by the pavilions at either end which have suggested William Kent (d. 1748) as their designer, by the modest swags on the plain balustrade above the Hippisley arms and by the four Tuscan columns and frieze of roses are a mask for the decoration within, now so splendidly restored. The modest hall leads to a symmetrical saloon, rightly acclaimed a fine specimen of its kind. The eagle of Jupiter emerges from the sun to look down from the fine ceiling. The entrance door is flanked by Corinthian columns supporting a frieze of wheat and vines. Pier glasses hang between the north-facing windows which give views down the steep scarp to the magnificent grounds and cascades beyond. Arcadian and Classical

Hippisley family retainers: an early 19th century painting brought back to the house by the present owners.

subjects painted in grisaille decorate the walls. Drawing room, dining room, library and print room (with cupboards reminiscent again of Kent) continue the Classical theme, for which there still survive drawings by the younger John Wood of Bath (d. 1782), although experts have also seen the hand of Thomas Paty of Bristol in some of the plaster ceilings and dados. There still remain at least two rooms decorated with the painted panelling which had been so fashionable a century earlier.

Richard Hippisley Coxe, the finisher of the mansion, died unmarried and a lunatic in 1786. His brother Henry succeeded and, continuing Richard's work, employed Humphrey Repton in 1793. Repton recognized the possibilities of that valley north of the house and his two weirs have recently been restored. Repton's schemes for tree planting to create vistas and woodland walks were obviously followed.

If Repton's work marked the end of the grand development of the house, it also marked the end of the Hippisley Coxes, but the death of Henry without children in 1795 brought the house under the control of a remarkable lady and of her genial though apparently rather pompous second husband, himself a descendant of another branch of the Hippisley family – Sir John Cox Hippisley was the

146 Ston Easton Park

husband, his lady Elizabeth Anne Horner, formerly of Mells, who survived Sir John and lived until 1843.

Memories of Elizabeth are still very much alive at Ston Easton. Her plunge bath occupies the eastern pavilion, next to the passage room where she prepared her famous herbal remedies. Some records of her regime survive among the family papers: 'the servants who are out with us at the Hall dinner time are to have each their meat served to them with their beer immediately after our dinner goes down and at no other time. No luncheons allowed. If unnecessarily unpunctual or unclean they are to go without any thing untill the next meal'.

The cellar and the gardens attracted her Ladyship's attention: in 1803 the household consumed 14 hogsheads of strong beers and she left instructions for 8 hogsheads to be brewed each half year. The great wine cellar in 1804 contained 243 dozen port, and since the average annual consumption was modest at 22 dozen there was plenty laid up. Winter and spring in their London home was another concern, and there were detailed requirements recorded for the delivery of food. In February 1806 the first waggon from the country was to bring up two porkers, rounds of brisket, joints of beef and flitches of bacon all at about 40 lbs each, and a basket of peas and onions. A second waggon was to include a 40 lb porker pig, french beans, celery, sea kale, and broccoli. Three baskets were to contain chicken, geese, hare, turkey, duck, parsley, radishes and salad.

There is more than a suspicion that Lady Hippisley interpreted her inheritance of her first husband's estate rather further than the law strictly allowed and removed Hippisley heirlooms from the house to her family home at Mells. That, at any rate, is an interpretation based on the poor survival of quality furniture and plate such as the builders of the mansion might be assumed to have possessed. Perhaps she did not approve the prospect of a distant and unsuitable branch of her husband's family taking over her domain. But on her death the house and estate passed to cousins by marriage so remote that they traced their claim as descendants of a younger brother of that John Hippisley who had died in 1664. So Lady Hippisley's heir at her death in 1843 was another John Hippisley, scion of the Lambourn Hippisleys.

John Hippisley was a remarkable man, a Fellow of the Royal Society and a pioneer photographer whose grandson and heir, Commander Richard John Bayntun Hippisley, followed in his footsteps. Richard's knowledge of the possibilities of wireless was put at the disposal of naval intelligence in the First World War and his workshop at Ston Easton remained until the 1950s the haven of an eccentric genius who, while a pioneer in motor vehicles and aircraft remained profoundly suspicious of the domestic uses of electricity and of the telephone. Post-war economics had taken their toll of the estate, which no longer could support the house. The lead disappeared from the roof and rainwater did its worst. Fittings were removed and only a preservation order issued in 1958 saved both

The fireplace in the ornate Saloon.

the building and its remaining contents.

Restoration has taken nearly thirty years and the expenditure of much care as well as money. Stephen Clark, William Rees-Mogg and now Peter and Christine Smedley have in their several ways saved the house and recreated its beauties. Today it is an elegant hotel, and the visitor is welcomed and cosseted and sustained by a staff whose standards of hospitality were set long ago when Lady Hippisley ruled. The painting of four of her servants which has been brought back to the house and now graces the dining room has its modern counterpart in a photograph of the entire staff who have, in some sense, recreated the affluence of the country house community in this elegant place.

Ven

A farm called Fene, the subject of a dispute in Star Chamber in Henry VIII's reign, had come in 1679 to be the manor of Venn or Venwick which Edward Carent sold to Sir Edward Carteret, Black Rod. Sir Edward's son Charles, who married one of Queen Mary of Modena's Maids of Honour, was interested in the political possibilities of nearby Milborne Port, for it returned two members to Parliament by a method peculiarly susceptible to manipulation. Sir Charles was duly returned by the borough electors to three Parliaments in the 1690s, presumably the result of his control of at least some of the nine 'capital burgages' whose tenants, each called a 'capital bailiff', served in pairs as returning officers each year and thus were in a position to play a crucial role in an election.

During his second term as one of the borough's members, in 1696, Carteret sold his manor of Ven to Thomas Medlycott, younger son of another Thomas, a lawyer by training, who had been M.P. for Abingdon, then in Berkshire. The elder Thomas was a man well versed in political 'arrangements' and electoral manipulation, not always to his own advantage, and himself had been the son of a prosperous London dyer.

The younger Thomas, a Tory in politics, was already a member of the Irish Parliament, and his acquisition of Ven gave him a seat for the borough of Milborne Port at the election of 1705, a seat which his older brother James occupied for twelve years from 1710 and which he himself took again in 1727.

The house which Thomas bought with Ven manor in 1696 remained until the 19th century, but a farmhouse was not a suitable dwelling for a manipulating politician. For many years the story was told that the new mansion was built in 1698-1700 for the sum of £2,492 6s. 4d. for James Medlycott. The summary building account on which that story was based has now again come to light and with the rest of the Medlycott papers is in the Somerset Record Office. It reveals both less and more than people have claimed.

The account is actually the work of two people, one concerned to record purchases of materials, another to discover the total cost. A third writer, probably arranging the family papers at a later date, added the words 'Cost of building Ven House outhouses etc in the year 1700 which was begun in 1698'. And so the story was born. The actual cost, according to the second 'scribe', was £2,895 8s. 4d., but he inadvertently misread some of the figures, and the correct

The south front and terrace, with
Decimus Burton's Conservatory of 1836.

total should have been £2,493 4s. 4d. It should be noted that
nowhere is the name of James Medlycott mentioned.

All this may seem at first irrelevant in a description of the surviving house, but such building details are rare at least for Somerset houses and so, too, is the name of the designer-builder which they contain. The man who for £1,050 had agreed with the owner for the work of carpenters, plumbers, bricklayers, and free- and rough-stone masons was 'Mr Ireson', Nathaniel Ireson from nearby Wincanton, who had worked for Colen Campbell at Stourhead in 1720 and whose work is still to be found in Somerset at Crowcombe Court (1734) and in Wincanton. But Ireson could not possibly have worked at Ven in 1698: he was then only twelve years old.

But by the time he came to Ven, 'Mr Ireson' was evidently a respected craftsman. Family tradition has it that Ireson was building for James Medlycott who, like many another, was ruined by the South Sea Bubble and still owed Ireson money at his death in 1731. A date in the 1720s seems likely for most of the work, though another account, submitted by William and Charles Issacke to James's brother Thomas in 1732 for black hearths and black fenders, one to

Thomas's own design, shows that internal work was still going on, and garden layouts for Thomas by Richard Grange were made later in the 1730s. It is just possible that the whole work was for the more prosperous Thomas.

Building work consumed 550,000 bricks at a cost of £467 10s, wheeled to the site for a further £27 10s; timber from Brewham Forest, Motcombe, Lord Digby's and the Medlycott estate; over 6,402 feet of stone from Doughthill (?Doulting) and Charlton. Ireson acted not only as contractor but also more directly: he received £30 'for the windows and doors at the west end (?) more you agreed' and £10 'for Ballington on the house more you agreed'. After the brick, timber and detailed carpenters' work was the more expensive part of the whole enterprise: the raw materials and carriage of timber amounted to £334 12s; oak for the outer doors cost £15; sashes, sash frames, pulley wheels and Crown glass for 71 windows cost a further £99 15s. The total cost is hidden: the lead for the roof and the freestone were already paid for.

The house gives the appearance of symmetry that cunningly disguises its oddities. One of those oddities is that while rectangular in plan it has seven bays on its main north and south fronts, six on the east, and five on the west: hence the 71 sash windows. It comprises a basement, two main storeys and attics, but the basement is masked on the south by a raised terrace. The whole is of brick, using about the ordered 550,000, with stone dressings, the main facades each divided by four pilasters with Corinthian capitals linking the two main storeys. Above a cornice the attic floor, topped by a balustrade, has pilasters marking each bay. The entrance (north) front originally

The north front with one of Burton's pavilions.

Richard Grange's plan for the south terrace and garden, showing two small pavilions and formal planting, c.1725.

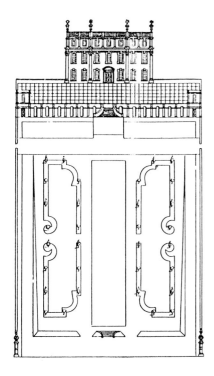

had no porch, but simply the scrolly pediment and columns now attached to a porch. The garden door has a segmental pediment.

North and south facades face formal gardens. The original entrance was along a drive through gates set in semicircular railings leading between a double avenue of trees and formal parterres to a second pair of gates where it divided to form an oval. From the paved terrace to the south, with small pavilions at its two outer corners, steps led down to a gravel walk and a long canal set in lawns with ornamental trees planted in geometric beds.

The Medlycotts built Ven as an outward and visible sign of their influence in Milborne Port, an influence which they shared at each general election with successive owners of the remaining capital burgages in a pact designed to save each the expense of a contest. Thus a Medlycott was returned to every Parliament without question until 1770. At a by-election in 1772 the Medlycott candidate actually lost on the first return but was seated on petition. Two years later the matter was even more confused, and doubtless expensive for the patrons, for the election came when the two capital burgesses were going out of office and two more were coming in. Both patrons put up two candidates each and three of the possible four returning officers sent in a different return. In the event both Medlycott candidates were victorious, thanks to a shady deal involving Lord North.

Thomas Hutchings Medlycott, who had upheld his family's tradition for nearly thirty years by the time of his death in 1795, was succeeded by his son William Coles Medlycott. He had sat briefly in Parliament in his father's lifetime but he took little interest in politics,

Above. An alas rather poor quality watercolour of the north entrance and the old farm buildings including the entrance arch and dovecote in 1835. The painting is one of two by Sarah, Lady Medlycott, wife of the 2nd Baronet, showing the house prior to the alterations.

Left. The central Hall after remodelling by Burton in 1836.

and conceded his political interest in Milborne Port to the Earl of Uxbridge and his heir Lord Paget. His reward was probably the baronetcy he received in 1808.

Soon after his death in 1835 his son, Sir W.C. Medlycott, made the first significant alteration to their home in a century by employing Decimus Burton to demolish the old farmhouse, remove the large, divided staircase from the rear of the central hall, replacing it with rooms, and to add detached offices to flank the east side of the house, balancing it with a large conservatory on the west side. The work, apparently carried out in 1836 by Thomas Cubitt, included the redecoration of the three reception rooms on the south side of the house.

In the 1890s Sir Edward Bradford Medlycott lavished care on the grounds, rather changed from their 18th-century style, a care which was shared by his son Sir Hubert, but the maintenance of such a property was becoming a considerable burden. The family had moved out by 1906, and in 1927 advertised for a tenant prepared to take on its sixteen bedrooms, large hall, four reception rooms, billiard room, and stabling for ten horses in a district where hunting could be had with eight packs of hounds. Tenants continued to be found until 1957 when the Medlycotts sold. Milborne Port had lost the right to send members to Parliament in 1832; the house had lost its purpose. Yet the house remains a focus of family interest and affection.

Woodspring Priory

The house of Augustinian canons dedicated to the Holy Trinity, St Mary and St Thomas the Martyr, was established in place of his manorial chapel by William de Courtenay in this remote part of North Somerset in the early years of the 13th century. If that was the full and formal dedication, Prior Roger Tormynton in 1536 was content to call his home the house of St Thomas the Martyr of Worspryng. That was the year the community was scattered. Prior Roger and his seven brethren had signed the declaration acknowledging the supremacy of His Majesty the King instead of His Holiness the Pope in 1534; and like many of his fellow canons and monks throughout the country they may well have been apprehensive for the future. It was a future in which outside pressures threatened to grow, in which the patronage of secular neighbours might be both vital and expensive. Thomas Horner's support brought in badly-needed money when he paid £50 for a fine for land he acquired on lease from the priory, but the land was thereby effectively lost for many years. Early in 1536 the canons actually sold outright a farm at Weston super Mare to trustees acting for William Oldmixon. By that time their numbers had fallen by one: Robert Coke who had been there in 1534 was not among them. Later in the year they left the house on which they and their predecessors had lavished such care.

Much of what they left still stands, on slightly rising ground sheltered from the north and with a splendid view across the flat grasslands to the wooded ridge where even then Worlebury camp was the oldest man-made feature in the landscape; and far beyond that, south-east across the marshes of the Axe river, to the Mendip scarp.

Perhaps its very remoteness was the salvation of so much of the fabric of the place. No-one lived near enough to use the buildings as a convenient quarry and still, more than four hundred years later, the two most substantial buildings on the site when Prior Tormynton and his brethren left stand proud and substantial. First is the seven-bay barn, only one of its central porches surviving, and now in the ownership of the National Trust. It is a hugely solid building, reflecting the importance of agriculture to the canons when they built it in the 15th century. The magnificent open roof is arch-braced with collars and windbraces, carefully copied in 1934 from the decaying originals. Around the barn, their sites now covered with modern agricultural buildings, must have been other structures. There is the

Opposite top. Tower and nave from the south, showing outline of original nave window.

Opposite bottom. The Priory Barn, restored in 1934.

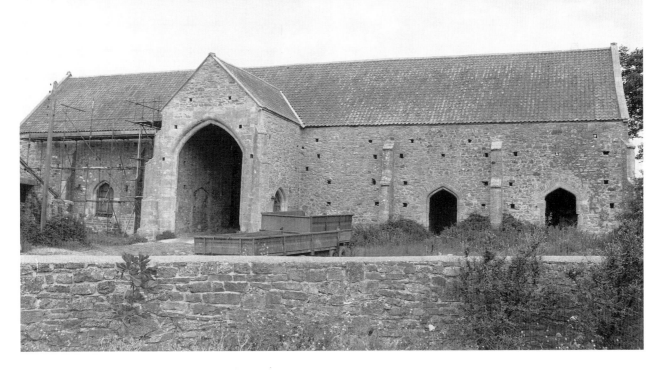

suggestion that cattle may have played an increasingly important part in the priory's economy in the Later Middle Ages. Certainly south of the barn were fishponds fed by one of the springs rising to the north of the site.

The other main structure to survive, and surely something of a surprise, is the priory church, or rather the nave, north aisle and crossing. Excavations have revealed much more – two successive choirs, a Lady chapel, and the outlines of the east cloister range, all now buried again under grass. Their story, however, is one repeated so many times, the story of a vast rebuilding undertaken in the late 15th and the early 16th century. The original 13th-century choir was under the new plan shortened by almost a half, for the first hopes for a substantial community had never been realised. The 14th-century Lady chapel on the south side of the choir was also abandoned. In their place the canons built a new choir, and at the same time built a slightly shorter nave. Between them rose a tower, to be seen for miles across the flat grassland. The nave, occupied as a dwelling from the Dissolution and still to be restored for public access, was evidently impressive. At its western corners were octagonal angle turrets flanking an enormous west window, only its outlines now visible. Inside, at its east end, once stood a richly-decorated stone screen and in front of it at least one altar. Here on 30 August 1525 the newly-chosen Prior Roger Tormynton was presented to a gathering assembled for this rare event although he exhibited suitable modesty and actually took another six hours to agree to accept the task.

By that time the tower was getting on for a century old, another example of the work of those prolific Somerset masons whose pierced Somerset tracery is in the tall three-light windows of the bell openings. Above is a pierced parapet once topped by pinnacles, their fellows still clinging to the corners above the diagonal buttresses.

The crossing under the tower between nave and chancel was the main entrance way for the community from cloister and dormitory to choir. The fine fan vault seems now to be the work of John Buckler in the early 19th century but it surely replaced similar work which matched the panelling and crocketing of the screen, now so sadly defaced. The south window, restored in 1970, was once filled with painted glass and would have been repeated throughout the building; and ghostly shapes of windows may still be traced in the final addition to the church, a north aisle which still bears traces of its richness. It was once roofed, too, with fan vaults, and it may well have been the site of a shrine of St Thomas, separated from the nave by wooden screens. The addition was almost certainly the work of Prior Richard Spryng, who was forced to retire in 1525 after ruling his house for thirty-four years. He was by that time over ninety years old.

South-east of the cloister is the infirmary, which perhaps had a chapel on its southern side. It was built in the early 15th century and

The tower vault restored by John Buckler in the 19th century.

A wash drawing by John Buckler dated 1829 showing the Church, Prior's Lodging and entrance arch from the south-west.

has a fine arch-braced roof with collars and windbraces. This, most of the church and another range running west from the new north aisle were soon after the closure of the house converted to a dwelling and to agricultural use. That western range, yet to be restored, bears the date 1701 over its central doorway on the southern side; but inside, already, has been found a 16th-century fireplace. Yet it probably incorporates the lodging of the prior before the Dissolution, and almost certainly included the room which Prior Spryng had occupied before his retirement, 'a fair chamber adjoining, with a cellar, a barn and a garden'. Presumably the range also included quarters for the new prior.

This range will surely reveal more secrets as the present owners, the Landmark Trust, continue to remove four centuries of confusion. When the end came first Humphrey Stafford, claiming as descendant of the founder, and then Edward Fetyplace came forward to purchase a lease of the buildings and adjoining meadows. Fetyplace was successful and it may be no accident that the former prior Tormynton was soon appointed to a secular living near Fetyplace's Berkshire home. Thomas Horner, already in possession of much of the rest of the estate, continued to take his profits for such time as his lease lasted; and another potential owner, the priory's former steward Sir John St Loe, acquired a reversionary lease of the priory site when Fetyplace's lease should expire. Just before that time the inevitable London entrepreneurs appeared. William and John Lacy, never actual owners, were nevertheless involved in a transaction in 1566 by which William Carre, a Bristol merchant, acquired 'the house and site late priory of Worspryng and church, belfry and cemetery of the same'. Already the buildings must have been adapted to secular use. And when in 1618 the property had come into the hands of Thomas Young from the Carres by marriage, the legal description makes that clear: 'house and site of the late priory of Worspryng and the manor or farm or grange of Worspryng'. It was already a working farm, but not yet a gentleman's residence. The Youngs lived miles to the east at Ogborne St George in Wiltshire. From William Young, Thomas's nephew, it passed in 1636 to Sir Ralph Hopton, later the Civil War commander. He, too, lived elsewhere, principally later in a house constructed from the remains of another former monastery, Witham.

The tower and north aisle from the east, where earthworks reveal the site of the former choir.

The ownership of Worspryng thereafter is less precisely known, but towards the end of the 17th century it came into the possession of the Smyth-Pigott family, Somerset gentry who may have used the former prior's residence as a dwelling. What had once been in a real sense the country house of successive priors was now perhaps reduced in height and remodelled. How long it could strictly be considered a country house is uncertain. As part of the vast Smyth-Pigott estate it was subsequently let to a succession of tenants and became the centre of a farm which by the late 19th century included a golf course. In 1918 the owners sold and the purchasers drew up grandiose plans, fortunately never fulfilled, to turn the house into a hotel as part of a suggested bungalow town, Somerset's Peacehaven. Farm and ruins are now protected from such ideas: the National Trust acquired the property in 1968 and since 1972 the Landmark Trust, while continuing its fine work of restoration, has welcomed the public to view part of the former church and to enjoy the haunting site of this house, so deep in the country. Some day, holiday makers will be able to occupy some of the fair rooms in the prior's lodging and imagine themselves, as successive priors, temporary owners of a country estate.

The Illustrations

Virtually all of the photographs in this book were specially taken by Anthony Kersting, to whom I am deeply indebted: their quality speaks for itself. I am also grateful to the following for allowing me to make use of illustrations in their possession or for which they hold the copyright: The National Trust, 44, 48. The Royal Institute of British Architects, 85. Somerset Natural History and Archaeological Society, 8 (top), 19 (top), 45 (bottom), 47 (top), 50, 51, 60 (top) 62, 80 (top), 84 (top), 94, 157. Mrs Christine J. Smedley, 145. Somerset County Library, 81 (top). Somerset County Council, 41 (top), 41 (bottom). Peter Hopkins Esq, 80 (bottom). G. Roberts Esq, 26. J.P.S. Dunning Esq, 38, 82 (right), 88 (top), 108 (top), 156. Royal Commission on the Historical Monuments of England, 20 (top), 20 (bottom), 70 (left), 70/71, 88 (bottom), 98, 108 (bottom), 149, 150, 151(top), 152. Somerset Record Office, 58 (bottom) 142 (bottom). The National Portrait Gallery, 22, 25, 37. Sir Mervyn Medlycott, 153. Michael McGarvie Esq, 91 (top). A.W. MacCaw Esq, 151 (bottom). Mrs Sophia Rawlins, 112 (top), 113 (bottom), 114 (top), 114 (bottom). David Burnett Esq, 8 (bottom), 10 (top), 10 (bottom), 11 (top), 24, 57 (top), 66/67, 69, 73, 79, 81 (bottom), 82 (left), 82 (bottom), 99, 109 (right), 136, 137 (top), 144, 155 (top), 155 (bottom), 158.